Bartlett's Book of
Love Quotations

Bartlett's Book of
Love Quotations

Compiled by Barbara Ann Kipfer

LITTLE, BROWN AND COMPANY
BOSTON   NEW YORK   TORONTO   LONDON

First Edition

Illustrations by Carol O'Malia

Library of Congress Cataloging-in-Publication Data

Bartlett's book of love quotations / compiled by Barbara Ann Kipfer.
— 1st ed.
      p.   cm.
  A thematic grouping of quotations from: Bartlett's familiar
quotations.
  ISBN: 0-316-08292-9
  1. Love — Quotations, maxims, etc.   I. Kipfer, Barbara Ann.
II. Barlett, John, 1820–1905. Familiar quotations.
PN6084.L6B37   1994
302.3 — dc20   93-27519

10 9 8 7 6 5 4 3 2 1

BP

*Published simultaneously in Canada
by Little, Brown & Company (Canada) Limited*

Printed in the United States of America

Contents

Romance

Music I heard with you was more
   than music,
And bread I broke with you was more
   than bread.
Now that I am without you, all is des-
   olate;
All that was once so beautiful is dead.

> Conrad Aiken
> "Bread and Music" [1914]

I both love and do not love, and am
   mad and am not mad.

> Anacreon
> Fragment 79

Oh, the days dwindle down
To a precious few . . .
And these few precious days
I'll spend with you.

> Maxwell Anderson
> *Knickerbocker Holiday* [1938]. Septem-
> ber Song

I am a lover and have not found my
   thing to love.

> Sherwood Anderson
> *Winesburg, Ohio* [1919]. Tandy

For in my mind, of all mankind
I love but you alone.

> Anonymous
> "The Nut-Brown Maid" [15th century],
> refrain

Frankie and Johnny were lovers, my
  gawd, how they could love,
Swore to be true to each other, true
  as the stars above;
He was her man, but he done her
  wrong.

> Anonymous
> "Frankie and Johnny," st. 1

I was more true to Love than Love
  to me.

> Anonymous
> From John Dowland, *The First Book of
> Songs or Airs* [1597]

I wooed her in the wintertime
And in the summer too;
And the only, only thing I did that
  was wrong
Was to keep her from the foggy, foggy
  dew.

> Anonymous
> "The Foggy, Foggy Dew," st. 1

Love not me for comely grace,
For my pleasing eye or face,
Nor for any outward part,
No, nor for a constant heart.

> Anonymous
> From John Wilbye, *Second Set of
>   Madrigals* [1609]

Over the mountains and over the
    waves,
Under the fountains and under the
    graves;
Under floods that are deepest, which
    Neptune obey,
Over rocks that are steepest, Love
    will find out the way.

> Anonymous
> "Love Will Find Out the Way," st. 1

Sabina has a thousand charms
To captivate my heart;
Her lovely eyes are Cupid's arms,
And every look a dart:
But when the beauteous idiot speaks,
She cures me of my pain;
Her tongue the servile fetters breaks
And frees her slave again.

> Anonymous
> From *Amphion Anglicus* [1700]

L'amour, l'amour fait tourner le
  monde [It's love, it's love that
  makes the world go round].

> Anonymous French song

Quien bien te quiere te har á llorar
  [Whoever really loves you will
  make you cry].

> Anonymous Spanish proverb

There is a lady sweet and kind,
Was never face so pleased my
  mind;
I did but see her passing by,
And yet I love her till I die.

> Anonymous
> From Thomas Ford, *Music of Sundry
> Kinds* [1607], st. 1

Cras amet qui nunquam amavit
  quique amavit cras amet [Tomor-
  row let him love who has never
  loved and tomorrow let him who
  has loved love].

> Anonymous Latin
> *Pervigilium Veneris* [c. 350], refrain

Creep into thy narrow bed,
Creep, and let no more be said!

> Matthew Arnold
> "The Last Word" [1867], st. 1

Ah, love, let us be true
To one another! for the world, which
  seems
To lie before us like a land of dreams,
So various, so beautiful, so new,
Hath really neither joy, nor love, nor
  light,
Nor certitude, nor peace, nor help for
  pain;
And we are here as on a darkling plain
Swept with confused alarms of strug-
  gle and flight,
Where ignorant armies clash by
  night.

> Arnold
> *Dover Beach* [1867], st. 3, 4

Lay your sleeping head, my love,
Human on my faithless arm.

> W. H. Auden
> "Lullaby" [1940], st. 1

The greater the love, the more false
  to its object,
Not to be born is the best for man;
After the kiss comes the impulse to
  throttle,
Break the embraces, dance while you
  can.

> Auden
> "O Who Can Ever Gaze His Fill"
> [1937]

I was in love with loving.

> Saint Augustine
> *Confessions* [397–401], III, 1

A lady's imagination is very rapid; it
  jumps from admiration to love,
  from love to matrimony in a moment.

> Jane Austen
> *Pride and Prejudice* [1813], ch. 6

Kiss till the cow comes home.

> Francis Beaumont and John Fletcher
> *The Scornful Lady* [1616], act III, sc. i

Of all the objects of hatred, a
   woman once loved is the most
   hateful.

> Max Beerbohm
> *Zuleika Dobson* [1911], ch. 13

Oh, what a dear ravishing thing is
   the beginning of an Amour!

> Aphra Behn
> *The Emperor of the Moon* [1687], act I,
> sc. i

The sort of girl I liked to see
Smiles down from her great height at
   me.

> John Betjeman
> "The Olympic Girl" [1954]

How much better is thy love than
   wine!

> The Bible
> Old Testament
> Song of Solomon 4:10

Jacob served seven years for Rachel;
  and they seemed unto him but a
  few days, for the love he had to
  her.

> Old Testament
> Genesis 29:20

Keep me as the apple of the eye,
  hide me under the shadow of thy
  wings.

> Old Testament
> Psalms 17:8

Rise up, my love, my fair one, and
  come away.
For, lo, the winter is past, the rain is
  over and gone;
The flowers appear on the earth;
  the time of the singing of birds is
  come, and the voice of the turtle
  is heard in our land.

> Old Testament
> Song of Solomon 2:10–12

Set me as a seal upon thine heart,
  as a seal upon thine arm: for love
  is strong as death; jealousy is
  cruel as the grave.

> Old Testament
> Song of Solomon 8:6

Thou art all fair, my love; there is
   no spot in thee.

> Old Testament
> Song of Solomon 4:7

Love seeketh not itself to please,
Nor for itself hath any care,
But for another gives its ease,
And builds a Heaven in Hell's de-
   spair.

> William Blake
> *Songs of Experience* [1794]. The Clod
> and the Pebble, st. 1

Love to faults is always blind,
Always is to joy inclin'd,
Lawless, wing'd, and unconfin'd,
And breaks all chains from every
   mind.

> Blake
> *Poems* [written c. 1791–1792] *from
> Blake's Notebook.* Love to Faults

The look of love alarms
Because 'tis fill'd with fire;
But the look of soft deceit
Shall win the lover's hire.

> Blake
> Ibid. Several Questions Answered, no.
> 2, The Look of Love

There is a smile of love,
And there is a smile of deceit,
And there is a smile of smiles
In which these two smiles meet.

> Blake
> *Poems from the Pickering Manuscript*
> [c. 1805]. The Smile, st. 1

What is it men in women do require?
The lineaments of Gratified Desire.
What is it women do in men require?
The lineaments of Gratified Desire.

> Blake
> *Poems from Blake's Notebook*. Several
> Questions Answered, no. 4, What Is
> It

Who can give law to lovers? Love is a greater law to itself.

> Boethius
> *De Consolatione Philosophiae*, bk. III,
> 12, 47

Breathless, we flung us on the
windy hill,
Laughed in the sun, and kissed the
lovely grass.

> Rupert Brooke
> "The Hill" [1910]

And love can come to everyone,
The best things in life are free.

> Lew Brown and Buddy De Silva
> *Good News* [1927]. The Best Things in
> Life Are Free

Sure there is music even in the
beauty, and the silent note which
Cupid strikes, far sweeter than
the sound of an instrument. For
there is a music wherever there is
a harmony, order, or proportion;
and thus far we may maintain the
music of the spheres.

> Sir Thomas Browne
> *Religio Medici* [1643], pt. II, sec. 9

How do I love thee? Let me count
  the ways.
I love thee to the depth and breadth
  and height
My soul can reach, when feeling out
  of sight
For the ends of Being and ideal
  Grace. . . .
        I love thee with the breath,
Smiles, tears, of all my life! — and, if
  God choose,
I shall but love thee better after
  death.

> Elizabeth Barrett Browning
> *Sonnets from the Portuguese* [1850],
>   no. 43

Escape me?
Never —
Beloved!
While I am I, and you are you.

> Robert Browning
> "Life in a Love" [1855]

        Only I discern
Infinite passion, and the pain
Of finite hearts that yearn.

> Browning
> "Two in the Campagna" [1855], st. 12

But to see her was to love her,
Love but her, and love forever.
Had we never lov'd sae kindly,
Had we never lov'd sae blindly,
Never met — or never parted —
We had ne'er been brokenhearted.

Robert Burns
Johnson's Musical Museum [1787–
1796]. Ae Fond Kiss, st. 2

O, my Luve is like a red, red rose,
That's newly sprung in June.
O, my Luve is like the melodie,
That's sweetly played in tune.

Burns
Ibid. A Red, Red Rose, st. 1

Had sigh'd to many, though he
loved but one.

Lord Byron
Childe Harold's Pilgrimage, canto I
[1812], st. 5

I only know we loved in vain;
I only feel — farewell! farewell!

Lord Byron
"Farewell! If Ever Fondest Prayer"
[1808], st. 2

She walks in beauty, like the night
Of cloudless climes and starry skies;
And all that's best of dark and bright
Meet in her aspect and her eyes:
Thus mellow'd to that tender light
Which heaven to gaudy day denies.

> Lord Byron
> *Hebrew Melodies* [1815]. She Walks in
> Beauty, st. 1

Man's love is of man's life a thing
  apart,
'Tis woman's whole existence.

> Lord Byron
> *Don Juan*, canto I [1818], st. 194

So we'll go no more a-roving
So late into the night,
Though the heart be still as loving,
And the moon be still as bright.

For the sword outwears its sheath,
And the soul wears out the breast,
And the heart must pause to breathe,
And love itself have rest.

Though the night was made for lov-
  ing,
And the day returns too soon,
Yet we'll go no more a-roving
By the light of the moon.

> Lord Byron
> "So We'll Go No More A-Roving"
> [1817]

The Devil hath not, in all his quiv-
   er's choice,
An arrow for the heart like a sweet
   voice.

> Lord Byron
> *Don Juan*, canto XV [1824], st. 13

There be none of Beauty's daugh-
   ters
With a magic like thee;
And like music on the waters
Is thy sweet voice to me.

> Lord Byron
> Stanzas for music [1816], st. 1

My sweetest Lesbia, let us live and
   love,
And though the sager sort our deeds
   reprove,
Let us not weigh them. Heaven's
   great lamps do dive
Into their west, and straight again re-
   vive,
But soon as once set is our little light,
Then must we sleep one ever-during
   night.

> Thomas Campion
> *A Book of Airs* [1601]. I

Never love unless you can
Bear with all the faults of man.

> Campion
> *Third Book of Airs* [1617]. XXVII

There is a garden in her face
Where roses and white lilies grow;
A heavenly paradise is that place
Wherein all pleasant fruits do flow.
There cherries grow which none may
    buy
Till "cherry-ripe" themselves do cry.

> Campion
> *Fourth Book of Airs* [1617]. VII, st. 1

Of all the girls that are so smart,
There's none like pretty Sally.
She is the darling of my heart,
And she lives in our alley.

> Henry Carey
> "Sally in Our Alley" [1729]. st. 1

He seems to me to be equal to a
   god, he, if it may be, seems to
   surpass the very gods, who sitting
   opposite you again gazes at you
   and hears you sweetly laughing.

> Catullus
> *Carmina*, LI, l. 1

Let us live and love, my Lesbia, and
   value at a penny all the talk of
   crabbed old men. Suns may set
   and rise again: for us, when our
   brief light has set, there's the
   sleep of perpetual night. Give me
   a thousand kisses.

> Catullus
> Ibid. V, l. 1

Over head and heels.

> Catullus
> Ibid. XX, l. 9

What a woman says to her ardent
    lover should be written in wind
    and running water.

> Catullus
> Ibid. LXX

I created you while I was happy,
    while I was sad,
with so many incidents, so many de-
    tails.

And, for me, the whole of you has
    been transformed into feeling.

> Constantine Peter Cavafy
> "In the Same Space" [1929]

Absence, that common cure of love.

> Miguel de Cervantes
> *Don Quixote de la Mancha*, pt. I
> [1605], bk. III, ch. 10

The eyes those silent tongues of
Love.

> Cervantes
> Ibid. II, 3

Love and War are the same thing,
and stratagems and policy are as
allowable in the one as in the
other.

> Cervantes
> Ibid. pt. II [1615], bk. III, ch. 21

Remember the old saying, "Faint
heart ne'er won fair lady."

> Cervantes
> Ibid, 10

[The tramp character:] A tramp, a
gentleman, a poet, a dreamer, a
lonely fellow, always hopeful of
romance and adventure.

> Charlie Chaplin
> *My Autobiography* [1964], ch. 10

              Cupido,
Upon his shuldres wynges hadde he
two;
And blynd he was, as it is often seene;
A bowe he bar and arwes brighte and
kene.

> Geoffrey Chaucer
> *Canterbury Tales* [c. 1387]. The
> Knight's Tale, l. 1963

For love is blynd.

> Chaucer
> Ibid. The Merchant's Tale, l.1598

One of the best things about love is just recognizing a man's step when he climbs the stairs.

> Colette
> *Occupation* [1941]

His heart runs away with his head.

> George Colman the Younger
> *Who Wants a Guinea?* [1805], act I,
> sc. i

Only a moment; a moment of strength, of romance, of glamour — of youth! . . . A flick of sunshine upon a strange shore, the time to remember, the time for a sigh, and — goodbye! — Night — Goodbye . . . !

> Joseph Conrad
> *Youth* [1902]

That faculty of beholding at a hint
   the face of his desire and the
   shape of his dream, without
   which the earth would know no
   lover and no adventurer.

> Conrad
> *Lord Jim* [1900], ch. 16

Sweet Genevieve,
The days may come, the days may go,
But still the hands of memory weave
The blissful dreams of long ago.

> George Cooper
> "Sweet Genevieve" [c. 1877]

Ye fields of Cambridge, our dear
   Cambridge, say,
Have ye not seen us walking every
   day?
Was there a tree about which did not
   know
The love betwixt us two?

> Abraham Cowley
> "On the Death of Mr. William Harvey"
> [1657]

And still to love, though prest with
   ill,
In wintry age to feel no chill,
With me is to be lovely still,
   My Mary!

> William Cowper
> "To Mary" [1791], st. 12

All in green went my love riding
on a great horse of gold
into the silver dawn.

> E. E. Cummings
> "All in green went my love riding"
> [1923]

Love hath so long possessed me for
   his own
And made his lordship so familiar.

> Dante Alighieri
> *La Vita Nuova* [1293]

Love with delight discourses in my
   mind
Upon my lady's admirable gifts . . .
Beyond the range of human intellect.

> Dante
> *Il Convito. Trattato Terzo,* l. 1

Love, which is quickly kindled in
the gentle heart, seized this man
for the fair form that was taken
from me, and the manner still
hurts me. Love, which absolves
no beloved one from loving,
seized me so strongly with his
charm that, as thou seest, it does
not leave me yet.

> Dante
> *The Divine Comedy* [c. 1310–1321].
> Inferno, canto V. l. 100

What sweet thoughts, what longing
led them to the woeful pass.

> Dante
> Ibid. Inferno, canto V, l. 113

Here lies a most beautiful lady,
Light of step and heart was she;
I think she was the most beautiful
lady
That ever was in the West Country.

> Walter de la Mare
> "An Epitaph"

That Love is all there is,
Is all we know of Love;
It is enough, the freight should be
Proportioned to the groove.

> Emily Dickinson
> No. 1765 [n.d.]

Dull sublunary lovers' love
(Whose soul is sense) cannot admit
Absence, because it doth remove
Those things which elemented it.

> John Donne
> "A Valediction Forbidding Mourning,"
>   st. 4

I am two fools, I know,
For loving, and for saying so
In whining poetry.

> Donne
> "The Triple Fool," st. 1

I long to talk with some old lover's
  ghost,
Who died before the god of love was
  born.

> Donne
> "Love's Deity," st. 1

Love's mysteries in souls do grow,
But yet the body is his book.

> Donne
> "The Extasy," l. 71

Sweetest love, I do not go,
For weariness of thee,
Nor in hope the world can show
A fitter love for me;
    But since that I
Must die at last, 'tis best,
To use my self in jest
  Thus by feign'd deaths to die.

> Donne
> Song ("Sweetest Love, I Do Not Go"),
>   st. 1

Take heed of loving me.

> Donne
> "The Prohibition," st. 1

Twice or thrice had I loved thee,
Before I knew thy face or name.

> Donne
> "Air and Angels," st. 1

So long as man remains free he strives for nothing so incessantly and so painfully as to find someone to worship.

Fëdor Dostoevski
The Brothers Karamazov [1879 –1880], bk. V, ch. 5

Pains of love be sweeter far
Than all other pleasures are.

John Dryden
Tyrannic Love [1669], act IV, sc. i

A difference of taste in jokes is a great strain on the affections.

George Eliot
Daniel Deronda [1876], bk. II, ch. 15

Let us go then, you and I,
When the evening is spread out
   against the sky
Like a patient etherized upon a table.

> T. S. Eliot
> "The Love Song of J. Alfred Prufrock"
> [1917]

Love is most nearly itself
When here and now cease to matter.
Old men ought to be explorers
Here and there does not matter
We must be still and still moving
Into another intensity
For a further union, a deeper com-
   munion
Through the dark cold and the empty
   desolation,
The wave cry, the wind cry, the vast
   waters
Of the petrel and the porpoise. In my
   end is my beginning.

> Eliot
> *Four Quartets.* East Coker [1940], V

Terminate torment
Of love unsatisfied
The greater torment
Of love satisfied.

> Eliot
> "Ash-Wednesday" [1930], II

Who then devised the torment?
 Love.
Love is the unfamiliar Name
Behind the hands that wove
The intolerable shirt of flame
Which human power cannot remove.
 We only live, only suspire
 Consumed by either fire or fire.

> Eliot
> *Four Quartets*. Little Gidding [1942],
> IV

Give all to love;
Obey thy heart;
Friends, kindred, days,
Estate, good fame,
Plans, credit and the Muse,
Nothing refuse.

> Ralph Waldo Emerson
> *Poems* [1847]. Give All to Love, st. 1

All mankind love a lover.

> Emerson
> *Essays: First Series* [1841]. Love

Thou art to me a delicious torment.

> Emerson
> Ibid. Friendship

Here's looking at you, kid.

> Julius J. Epstein, Philip G. Epstein,
> and Howard Koch
> *Casablanca* (screenplay) [1943]

Of all the gin joints in all the towns
in all the world, she walks into
mine!

> Epstein, Epstein, and Koch
> Ibid.

How a little love and good company
improves a woman!

> George Farquhar
> *The Beaux' Stratagem* [1707], act IV,
> sc. i

Love and scandal are the best
sweeteners of tea.

> Henry Fielding
> *Love in Several Masques* [1743]

A Book of Verses underneath the
   Bough,
A Jug of Wine, a Loaf of Bread
   — and Thou
Beside me singing in the Wilder-
   ness —
Oh, Wilderness were Paradise enow!

> Edward FitzGerald
> *The Rubáiyát of Omar Khayyám* [1879],
> st. 12

I dream of Jeanie with the light
   brown hair,
Floating, like a vapor, on the soft
   summer air.

> Stephen Foster
> "Jeanie with the Light Brown Hair"
> [1854], st. 1

To love and to work.

> Sigmund Freud
> From Erik H. Erikson, *Childhood and
> Society* [1963]

Love at the lips was touch
As sweet as I could bear;
And once that seemed too much;
I lived on air.

> Robert Frost
> "To Earthward" [1923], st. 1

Try thinking of love or something.
Amor vincit insomnia.

> Christopher Fry
> *A Sleep of Prisoners* [1951]

If the heart of a man is depress'd
    with cares,
The mist is dispelled when a woman
    appears.

> John Gay
> *The Beggar's Opera* [1728], act II, sc.
>   iii, air 21

If with me you'd fondly stray,
Over the hills and far away.

> Gay
> Ibid. act I, sc. xiii, air 16

'S wonderful! 'S marvelous —
You should care for me!

> Ira Gershwin
> *Funny Face* [1927]. 'S Wonderful

I got rhythm,
I got music,
I got my man —
Who could ask for anything more?

> Gershwin
> *Girl Crazy* [1930]. I Got Rhythm

Of thee I sing, baby,
You have got that certain thing, baby,
Shining star and inspiration
Worthy of a mighty nation,
Of thee I sing!

> Gershwin
> *Of Thee I Sing* [1931], title song

Oh, lady be good
To me.

> Gershwin
> *Lady Be Good* [1924]. Oh, Lady Be
> Good

The memory of all that —
No, no! They can't take that away
from me.

> Gershwin
> *Shall We Dance* [1937]. They Can't
> Take That Away from Me

Love Is Sweeping the Country.

> Gershwin
> *Of Thee I Sing*, title of song

I sighed as a lover, I obeyed as a
   son.

> Edward Gibbon
> *Memoirs (Autobiography)* [1796]

Faint heart never won fair lady!
Nothing venture, nothing win —
Blood is thick, but water's thin —
In for a penny, in for a pound —
It's Love that makes the world go
   round!

> Sir William S. Gilbert
> *Iolanthe* [1882], act II

It's a song of a merryman, moping
   mum,
Whose soul was sad, and whose
   glance was glum,
Who sipped no sup, and who craved
   no crumb,
As he sighed for the love of a lady.

> Gilbert
> *The Yeomen of the Guard* [1888], act I

Though the Philistines may jostle, you will rank as an apostle in the high aesthetic band,
If you walk down Piccadilly with a poppy or a lily in your medieval hand.
And everyone will say,
As you walk your flowery way,
"If he's content with a vegetable love, which would certainly not suit
    me,
Why, what a most particularly pure young man this pure young man must be!"

> Gilbert
> Ibid.

You must lie upon the daisies and discourse in novel phrases of your complicated state of mind,
The meaning doesn't matter if it's only idle chatter of a transcendental kind.
And everyone will say,
As you walk your mystic way,
"If this young man expresses himself in terms too deep for *me,*
Why, what a very singularly deep young man this deep young man must be!"

> Gilbert
> *Patience* [1881], act I

Twenty love-sick maidens we,
Love-sick all against our will.

> Gilbert
> Ibid.

While this magnetic,
Peripatetic
Lover he lived to learn,
By no endeavor,
Can magnet ever
Attract a silver churn!

> Gilbert
> Ibid. II

If I love you, what business is it of
yours?

> Johann Wolfgang von Goethe
> *Wilhelm Meister's Apprenticeship*
> [1786 –1830], bk. IV, ch. 9

All his faults are such that one loves
   him still the better for them.

> Oliver Goldsmith
> *The Good-Natur'd Man* [1768], act I

Can't help lovin' that man of mine.

> Oscar Hammerstein II
> *Show Boat* [1927]. Can't Help Lovin'
> That Man

Some enchanted evening . . .
You may see a stranger
Across a crowded room.

> Hammerstein
> *South Pacific* [1949]. Some Enchanted
> Evening

The last time I saw Paris, her heart
   was warm and gay.
I heard the laughter of her heart in
   every street café.

> Hammerstein
> "The Last Time I Saw Paris" [1940]

I'm Gonna Wash That Man Right Outa My Hair.

> Hammerstein
> *South Pacific*. Title of song

There Is Nothing Like a Dame.

> Hammerstein
> Ibid.

A lover without indiscretion is no lover at all.

> Thomas Hardy
> *The Hand of Ethelberta* [1876]

But sometimes a woman's love of being loved gets the better of her conscience.

> Hardy
> *Jude the Obscure* [1895], pt. IV, ch. 5

Child, you are like a flower,
So sweet and pure and fair.
I look at you, and sadness
Touches me with a prayer.

> Heinrich Heine
> *Du bist wie eine Blume*

On wings of song, my dearest,
I will carry you off.

> Heine
> *Auf Flügeln des Gesanges*

Every woman is the gift of a world
to me.

> Heine
> *Ideas: The Book Le Grand*

Love, and a cough, cannot be hid.

> George Herbert
> *Jacula Prudentum* [1651], no. 49

Bid me to live, and I will live
Thy Protestant to be,
Or bid me love, and I will give
A loving heart to thee.

> Robert Herrick
> *Hesperides* [1648]. To Anthea, Who
> May Command Him Any Thing

Give me a kiss, and to that kiss a
score;
Then to that twenty, add a hundred
more:
A thousand to that hundred: so kiss
on,
To make that thousand up a million.
Treble that million, and when that is
done,
Let's kiss afresh, as when we first be-
gun.

> Herrick
> Ibid. To Anthea: Ah, My Anthea!

So when you or I are made
A fable, song, or fleeting shade,
All love, all liking, all delight
Lies drowned with us in endless
night.

> Herrick
> Ibid. Corinna's Going A-Maying

What is a kiss? Why this, as some
approve:
The sure, sweet cement, glue, and
lime of love.

> Herrick
> Ibid. A Kiss

Whenas in silks my Julia goes,
Then, then (methinks) how sweetly
flows
That liquefaction of her clothes.

Next, when I cast mine eyes and see
That brave vibration each way free;
Oh how that glittering taketh me!

> Herrick
> Ibid. Upon Julia's Clothes

You say to me-wards your affection's strong;
Pray love me little, so you love me
long.

> Herrick
> Ibid. Love Me Little, Love Me Long

From their eyelids as they glanced
   dripped love.

     Hesiod
     The Theogony, l. 910

On his tongue they pour sweet dew,
   and from his mouth flow gentle
   words.

     Hesiod
     Ibid. l. 83

A hard beginning maketh a good
   ending.

     John Heywood
     Proverbs [1546], pt. I, ch. 4

Nothing is impossible to a willing
   heart.

     Heywood
     Ibid.

I'll woo her as the lion woos his
   brides.

> John Home
> *Douglas* [1756], act I, sc. i

She [Aphrodite] spoke and loosened
   from her bosom the embroidered
   girdle of many colors into which
   all her allurements were fash-
   ioned. In it was love and in it desire and in it blandishing
   persuasion which steals the mind
   even of the wise.

> Homer
> *The Iliad*, bk. XIV, l. 214

Oh, when I was in love with you,
Then I was clean and brave,
And miles around the wonder grew
How well I did behave.

And now the fancy passes by,
And nothing will remain,
And miles around they'll say that I
Am quite myself again.

> A. E. Housman
> *A Shropshire Lad* [1896], no. 18, st.
>   1–2

The supreme happiness of life is
the conviction that we are loved.

> Victor Hugo
> *Les Misérables* [1862]. Fantine, bk. V,
> ch. 4

You must remember this, a kiss is
   still a kiss,
A sigh is just a sigh;
The fundamental things apply,
As time goes by.

It's still the same old story,
A fight for love and glory,
A case of do or die!
The world will always welcome
   lovers,
As time goes by.

> Herman Hupfeld
> *Everybody's Welcome* [1931]. As Time
> Goes By

A woman's whole life is a history of
the affections.

> Washington Irving
> *The Sketch-Book* [1819–1820]. The
> Broken Heart

"Nothing, so it seems to me," said
   the stranger, "is more beautiful
   than the love that has weathered
   the storms of life. . . . The love
   of the young for the young, that is
   the beginning of life. But the love
   of the old for the old, that is the
   beginning of — of things longer."

> Jerome K. Jerome
> *The Passing of the Third Floor Back*
> [1908]

Come my Celia, let us prove,
While we can, the sports of love;
Time will not be ours forever,
He at length our good will sever.
Spend not then his gifts in vain;
Suns that set may rise again,
But if once we lose this light,
'Tis with us perpetual night.

> Ben Jonson
> "Song. To Celia" [1607]

I shall love you in December
With the love I gave in May!

> John Alexander Joyce
> "Question and Answer," st. 8

Where love rules, there is no will to power; and where power predominates, there love is lacking. The one is the shadow of the other.

> Jung
> From *Psychological Reflections: A Jung Anthology* [1953], p. 87: vol. 7, *The Psychology of the Unconscious* [1943]

A hope beyond the shadow of a dream.

> Keats
> *Endymion* [1818], bk. I, l. 857

The meeting of two personalities is like the contact of two chemical substances: if there is any reaction, both are transformed.

> Carl Jung
> *Modern Man in Search of a Soul* [1933]

A bright torch, and a casement ope at night,
To let the warm Love in!

> John Keats
> *Poems* [1820]. Ode to Psyche, st. 5

A virgin purest lipp'd, yet in the lore
Of love deep learned to the red
   heart's core.

   Keats
   Poems. Lamia, pt. I, l. 189

Beyond a mortal man impassion'd
   far
At these voluptuous accents, he
   arose,
Ethereal, flush'd, and like a throb-
   bing star
Seen mid the sapphire heaven's deep
   repose;
Into her dream he melted, as the
   rose,
Blendeth its odour with the vio-
   let, —
Solution sweet: meantime the frost-
   wind blows
Like Love's alarum pattering the
   sharp sleet
Against the window-panes; St.
   Agnes' moon hath set.

   Keats
   Ibid. The Eve of St. Agnes, st. 36

And they are gone: aye, ages long
　ago
These lovers fled away into the
　storm.

> Keats
> Ibid. st. 42

Forever wilt thou love, and she be
　fair!

> Keats
> Ibid. Ode on a Grecian Urn, st. 2

Love in a hut, with water and a
　crust,
Is — Love, forgive us! — cinders,
　ashes, dust.

> Keats
> Ibid. Lamia, pt. II, l.1

She looked at me as she did love,
And made sweet moan.

> Keats
> *Life, Letters and Literary Remains of*
> *John Keats,* ed. Richard Monckton
> Milnes [1848]. La Belle Dame Sans
> Merci, st. 5

I have two luxuries to brood over in
my walks, your Loveliness and
the hour of my death. Oh that I
could have possession of them
both in the same minute.

> Keats
> To Fanny Brawne [July 25, 1819]

'Tis the pest
Of love, that fairest joys give most un-
rest.

> Keats
> *Endymion*, bk. II, l. 365

Thou art the book,
The library whereon I look.

> Henry King
> "The Exequy" [1657]

God grant you find one face there
You loved when all was young!

> Charles Kingsley
> *Water Babies* [1863]. Song II, st. 1

Some say that the age of chivalry is past, that the spirit of romance is dead. The age of chivalry is never past, so long as there is a wrong left unredressed on earth, or a man or woman left to say, I will redress that wrong, or spend my life in the attempt.

> Kingsley
> From *Charles Kingsley: His Letters and Memories of His Life* [1879], vol. II, ch. 28

Absence diminishes mediocre passions and increases great ones, as the wind blows out candles and fans fire.

> François, Duc de La Rochefoucauld
> *Reflections; or, Sentences and Moral Maxims* [1678], maxim 276

In their first passion women love their lovers, in the others they love love.

> La Rochefoucauld
> Ibid. maxim 471

Lovers never get tired of each other, because they are always talking about themselves.

> La Rochefoucauld
> Ibid. maxim 312

The mind is always the dupe of the heart.

> La Rochefoucauld
> Ibid. maxim 102

There are very few people who are not ashamed of having been in love when they no longer love each other.

> La Rochefoucauld
> Ibid. maxim 71

True love is like ghosts, which everybody talks about and few have seen.

> La Rochefoucauld
> Ibid. maxim 76

Sex and beauty are inseparable, like life and consciousness. And the intelligence which goes with sex and beauty, and arises out of sex and beauty, is intuition.

> D. H. Lawrence
> "Sex Versus Loveliness" [1930]

I loved you, so I drew these tides of men into my hands and wrote my will across the sky in stars.
To earn you Freedom, the seven-pillared worthy house, that your eyes might be shining for me
When we came.

> T. E. Lawrence
> *Seven Pillars of Wisdom* [1926], dedication

I'll tell you something
I think you'll understand,
Then I'll say that something,
I want to hold your hand.

> John Lennon and Paul McCartney
> "I Want to Hold Your Hand" [1963]

It is easier to resist at the beginning
than at the end.

> Leonardo da Vinci
> *The Notebooks* [1508–1518], vol. I,
> ch. 2

I've grown accustomed . . . to her
face.

> Alan Jay Lerner
> *My Fair Lady* [1956]. I've Grown Ac-
> customed to Her Face

A woman without a man cannot
meet a man, any man, of any age,
without thinking, even if it's for a
half-second, Perhaps this is *the*
man.

> Doris Lessing
> *The Golden Notebook* [1962]. Free
> Women, 5

What is love? . . . It is the morning
and the evening star.

> Sinclair Lewis
> *Elmer Gantry* [1927], ch. 20

Farewell to thee, farewell to
  thee . . .
Until we meet again.

> Lydia Kamekeha Liliuokalani
> "Aloha Oe" (Farewell to Thee) [1878]

Love in my bosom like a bee
Doth suck his sweet.

> Thomas Lodge
> *Rosalynde* [1590]

I'd love to get you
On a slow boat to China.
All to myself alone.

> Frank Loesser
> "On a Slow Boat to China" [1948]

If I am not worth the wooing, I
  surely am not worth the winning.

> Henry Wadsworth Longfellow
> *The Courtship of Miles Standish* [1858],
>   pt. III

My love for you is mixed throughout
my body . . .

So hurry to see your lady,
like a stallion on the track,
or like a falcon swooping down to its
papyrus marsh.

Heaven sends down the love of her
as a flame falls in the hay.

Love Songs of the New Kingdom
Song no. 2

Now must I depart from the
brother . . .
and as I long for your love,
my heart stands still inside me. . . .

Sweet pomegranate wine in my
mouth
is bitter as the gall of birds.

But your embraces
alone give life to my heart;
may Amun give me what I have found
for all eternity.

Love Songs of the New Kingdom
Song no. 12

After loving you so much, can I forget
you for eternity, and have no other
choice?

> Robert Lowell
> "Obit" [1973]

I am glad that my Adonis hath a
sweet tooth in his head.

> John Lyly
> *Euphues and His England* [1580], p.
> 308

On Richmond Hill there lives a lass
More bright than Mayday morn;
Whose charms all other maids' sur-
pass —
A rose without a thorn.

> Leonard MacNally
> "The Lass of Richmond Hill," st. 1

All ye that be lovers call unto your remembrance the month of May, like as did Queen Guenever, for whom I make here a little mention, that while she lived she was a true lover, and therefore she had a good end.

> Sir Thomas Malory
> *Le Morte d'Arthur* [1485], bk. XVIII, ch. 25

And I will make thee beds of roses
And a thousand fragrant posies.

> Christopher Marlowe
> "The Passionate Shepherd to His Love" [c. 1589]

Oh, thou art fairer than the evening air
Clad in the beauty of a thousand stars.

> Marlowe
> *The Tragical History of Doctor Faustus* [1604], act V, sc. i

Was this the face that launched a
  thousand ships,
And burnt the topless towers of
  Ilium?
Sweet Helen, make me immortal
  with a kiss.
Her lips suck forth my soul; see,
  where it flies!

> Marlowe
> Ibid.

Who ever loved that loved not at
  first sight?

> Marlowe
> *Hero and Leander* [1598]

I love you as New Englanders love
  pie!

> Don Marquis
> *Sonnets to a Red-Haired Lady* [1922],
> XII

You ask what a nice girl will do?
  She won't give an inch, but she
  won't say no.

> Martial
> Epigrams, IV, 71

My love is of a birth as rare
As 'tis for object strange and high;
It was begotten by despair
Upon impossibility.

> Andrew Marvell
> "The Definition of Love" [1650–1652],
> st. 1

As lines, so loves oblique, may well
Themselves in every angle greet;
But ours, so truly parallel,
Though infinite, can never meet.

> Marvell
> Ibid. st. 7

I am Anne Rutledge who sleep beneath these weeds,
Beloved in life of Abraham Lincoln.

> Edgar Lee Masters
> *Spoon River Anthology* [1915]. Anne
> Rutledge

If you wish,
I shall grow irreproachably tender:
Not a man, but a cloud in trousers!

> Vladimir Mayakovski
> "Cloud in Trousers" [1915]

She whom I love is hard to catch
and conquer,
Hard, but O the glory of the winning
were she won!

George Meredith
"Love in the Valley" [1883], st. 2

The power of one fair face makes
my love sublime, for it weaned
my heart from low desires.

Michelangelo
Sonnet

Love is not all: it is not meat nor
drink
Nor slumber nor a roof against the
rain;
Nor yet a floating spar to men that
sink.

Edna St. Vincent Millay
"Love Is Not All" [1931], l. 1

A heaven on earth.

John Milton
Paradise Lost [1667], bk. IV, l. 208

So dear I love him, that with him all deaths
I could endure, without him live no life.

Milton
Ibid. bk. IX, l. 832

Freely we serve,
Because we freely love, as in our will
To love or not; in this we stand or fall.

Milton
Ibid. bk. V, l. 538

I'll think of some way to get him back. After all, tomorrow is another day.

Margaret Mitchell
Gone With the Wind [1936], pt. V, last line

If you press me to say why I loved him, I can say no more than it was because he was he and I was I.

Michel de Montaigne
Essays, bk. I [1580], ch. 28

But there's nothing half so sweet in
  life
As love's young dream.

> Thomas Moore
> *Irish Melodies* [1807–1834]. Love's
>   Young Dream, st. 1

I'll come to thee by moonlight,
  though hell should bar the way.

> Alfred Noyes
> "The Highwayman"

Amo, amas,
I love a lass,
As a cedar tall and slender;
Sweet cowslip's grace
Is her nominative case,
And she's of the feminine gender!

> John O'Keeffe
> *The Agreeable Surprise* [1783], act II,
>   sc. ii, Song

This night of no moon
There is no way to meet him.
I rise in longing —
My breast pounds, a leaping flame,
My heart is consumed in fire.

> Ono no Komachi
> *Kokinshu* [9th century]

Every lover is a warrior, and Cupid has his camps.

> Ovid
> *Amores*, I, ix, 1

To be loved, be lovable.

> Ovid
> *Ars Amatoria*, II, 107

Let those love now who never loved before;
Let those who always loved, now love the more.

> Thomas Parnell
> Translation of the *Pervigilium Veneris*

The heart has its reasons which reason knows nothing of.

> Blaise Pascal
> *Pensées* [1670], no. 277

Musick and women I cannot but
    give way to, whatever my busi-
    ness is.

> Samuel Pepys
> *Diary*, March 9, 1666

To be able to say how much you
    love is to love but little.

> Petrarch
> "To Laura in Death," canzone 137

Things are always at their best in
    their beginning.

> Pascal
> *Lettres provinciales* [1656–1657], no. 4

I do my thing, and you do your
    thing . . .
You are you and I am I,
And if by chance we find each other,
    it's beautiful;
If not, it can't be helped.

> Frederick Perls
> "Gestalt Therapy Verbatim" [1969]

I was a child and *she* was a child,
In this kingdom by the sea,
But we loved with a love that was
   more than love —
I and my Annabel Lee —
With a love that the wingèd seraphs
   of Heaven
Coveted her and me.

   Edgar Allan Poe
   "Annabel Lee" [1849], st. 2

And this maiden she lived with no
   other thought
Than to love and be loved by me.

   Poe
   Ibid. st. 1

Is it, in Heav'n, a crime to love too
   well?
To bear too tender, or too firm a
   heart,
To act a lover's or a Roman's part?
Is there no bright reversion in the sky,
For those who greatly think, or
   bravely die?

   Alexander Pope
   "Elegy to the Memory of an Unfortu-
   nate Lady" [1717], l. 6

Ye Gods! annihilate but space and
    time,
And make two lovers happy.

> Pope
> *Martinus Scriblerus on the Art of Sink-
>   ing in Poetry* [1728], ch. 11

But I'm always true to you, darlin',
    in my fashion,
Yes, I'm always true to you, darlin', in
    my way.

> Cole Porter
> *Kiss Me, Kate* [1948]. Always True to
>   You in My Fashion

I get no kick from champagne.
Mere alcohol doesn't thrill me at all,
So tell me why should it be true
That I get a kick out of you.

> Porter
> *Anything Goes* [1934]. I Get a Kick Out
>   of You

Night and day you are the one,
Only you beneath the moon and
    under the sun.

> Porter
> *Gay Divorce* [1932]. Night and Day

You do something to me
Something that simply mystifies me.

Porter
Fifty Million Frenchmen [1929]. You
   Do Something to Me

You're the Nile,
You're the Tower of Pisa,
You're the smile
On the Mona Lisa. . . .
But if, Baby, I'm the bottom you're
   the top!

Porter
Anything Goes [1934]. You're the Top!

Love me tender, love me sweet,
Never let me go.

Elvis Presley (with Vera Matson)
"Love Me Tender" [1956]

Be to her virtues very kind;
Be to her faults a little blind;
Let all her ways be unconfin'd;
And clap your padlock — on her
   mind!

Matthew Prior
An English Padlock [1707]

Absence makes the heart grow
  fonder.

> Sextus Propertius
> *Elegies*, II, xxxiii, 43

Love passed, the muse appeared,
  the weather
of mind got clarity newfound;
now free, I once more weave together
emotion, thought, and magic sound.

> Alexander Pushkin
> *Eugene Onegin* [1823], ch. 2, st. 59

But true love is a durable fire,
In the mind ever burning,
Never sick, never old, never dead,
From itself never turning.

> Sir Walter Ralegh
> "As You Came from the Holy Land"
>   [c. 1599], st. 11

Ain't misbehavin',
I'm savin' my love for you.

> Andy Razaf
> "Ain't Misbehavin' " [1929]

Love consists in this, that two soli-
  tudes protect and touch and greet
  each other.

> Rainer Maria Rilke
> *Letters to a Young Poet*

There is only one happiness in life,
  to love and be loved.

> George Sand
> Letter to Lina Calamatta [March 31,
> 1862]

O tender yearning, sweet hoping!
The golden time of first love!
The eye sees the open heaven,
The heart is intoxicated with bliss;
O that the beautiful time of young
  love
Could remain green forever.

> Friedrich von Schiller
> "The Song of the Bell" [1799]

Oh, promise me that some day you
    and I
Will take our love together to some
    sky
Where we can be alone and faith re-
    new,
And find the hollows where those
    flowers grew.

> Clement W. Scott
> "Oh, Promise Me" [1888]

Love means not ever having to say
    you're sorry.

> Erich Segal
> *Love Story* [1970]

Leaving the page of the book care-
    lessly open,
something unsaid, the phone off the
    hook
and the love, whatever it was, an in-
    fection.

> Anne Sexton
> "Wanting to Die" [1966], last stanza

Julia: They do not love that do not
show their love.
Lucetta: O! they love least that let
men know their love.

William Shakespeare
The Two Gentlemen of Verona, act I,
sc. ii, l. 31

Romeo: Lady, by yonder blessed
moon I swear
That tips with silver all these fruit-
tree tops —
Juliet: O! swear not by the moon, the
inconstant moon,
That monthly changes in her circled
orb,
Lest that thy love prove likewise vari-
able.

Shakespeare
Romeo and Juliet, act II, sc. ii, l. 107

. . . Do not swear at all;
Or, if thou wilt, swear by thy gracious
self,
Which is the god of my idolatry.

Shakespeare
Ibid. l. 112

All orators are dumb when beauty
pleadeth.

Shakespeare
The Rape of Lucrece, l. 268

But love is blind, and lovers cannot
see
The pretty follies that themselves
commit.

Shakespeare
The Merchant of Venice, act II, sc. vi,
l. 36

A pair of star-cross'd lovers.

Shakespeare
Ibid. prologue, l. 6

But I will wear my heart upon my
sleeve
For daws to peck at.

Shakespeare
Othello, act I, sc. i, l. 64

But love, first learned in a lady's eyes,
Lives not alone immured in the brain.

> Shakespeare
> *Love's Labour's Lost*, act IV, sc. iii, l. 327

For stony limits cannot hold love out.

> Shakespeare
> *Romeo and Juliet*, act ii, sc. ii, l. 67

From the east to western Ind,
No jewel is like Rosalind.

> Shakespeare
> *As You Like It*, act III, sc. ii, l. 94

Good night, good night! parting is such sweet sorrow,
That I shall say good night till it be morrow.

> Shakespeare
> *Romeo and Juliet*, act ii, sc. ii, l. 184

He is the half part of a blessed man,
Left to be finished by such a she;
And she is a fair divided excellence,
Whose fullness of perfection lies in
   him.

> Shakespeare
> *King John*, act II, sc. i, l. 437

He jests at scars, that never felt a
   wound.
But, soft! what light through yonder
   window breaks?
It is the east, and Juliet is the sun!

> Shakespeare
> *Romeo and Juliet*, act II, sc. ii, l. 1

Hereafter, in a better world than
   this,
I shall desire more love and knowledge of you.

> Shakespeare
> *As You Like It*, act I, sc. ii, l. 301

How silver-sweet sound lovers'
   tongues by night,
Like softest music to attending ears!

> Shakespeare
> *Romeo and Juliet*, act II, sc. ii, l. 165

I humbly do beseech you of your
  pardon
For too much loving you.

> Shakespeare
> *Othello*, act III, sc. iii, l. 212

I lov'd Ophelia: forty thousand
  brothers
Could not, with all their quantity of
  love,
Make up my sum.

> Shakespeare
> *Hamlet*, act V, sc. i, l. 291

It is too rash, too unadvis'd, too sud-
  den;
Too like the lightning, which doth
  cease to be
Ere one can say it lightens.

> Shakespeare
> *Romeo and Juliet*, act II, sc. ii, l. 118

It was a lover and his lass,
With a hey, and a ho, and a hey
   nonino,
That o'er the green corn-field did
   pass,
In the spring time, the only pretty
   ring time,
When birds do sing, hey ding a ding,
   ding;
Sweet lovers love the spring.

> Shakespeare
> *As You Like It*, act V, sc. iii, l. 18

Journeys end in lovers meeting,
Every wise man's son doth know.

> Shakespeare
> *Twelfth-Night*, act II, sc. iii, l. 46

Kindness in women, not their beauteous looks,
Shall win my love.

> Shakespeare
> *The Taming of the Shrew*, act IV, sc. ii,
> l. 41

Love comforteth like sunshine after
rain.

> Shakespeare
> *Venus and Adonis*, l. 799

Love goes toward love, as school-
  boys from their books;
But love from love, toward school
  with heavy looks.

> Shakespeare
> *Romeo and Juliet*, act II, sc. ii, l. 156

Love looks not with the eyes, but
  with the mind,
And therefore is wing'd Cupid
  painted blind.

> Shakespeare
> *A Midsummer-Night's Dream*, act I,
> sc. i, l. 234

Love sought is good, but giv'n un-
  sought is better.

> Shakespeare
> *Twelfth-Night,* act III, sc. i, l. 170

My man of men.

> Shakespeare
> *Antony and Cleopatra*, act I, sc. v, l. 71

My only love sprung from my only
  hate!
Too early seen unknown, and known
  too late!

> Shakespeare
> *Romeo and Juliet*, act I, sc. v, l. 142

See! how she leans her cheek upon
  her hand:
O! that I were a glove upon that hand,
That I might touch that cheek.

> Shakespeare
> Ibid. act II, sc. ii, l. 23

Shall I compare thee to a summer's
  day?
Thou art more lovely and more tem-
  perate:
Rough winds do shake the darling
  buds of May,
And summer's lease hath all too short
  a date.

> Shakespeare
> Sonnet 18, l. 1

She's beautiful and therefore to be
   woo'd,
She is a woman, therefore to be won.

> Shakespeare
> *King Henry the Sixth, Part I*, act V, sc.
> iii, l. 78

The iron tongue of midnight hath
   told twelve;
Lovers, to bed; 'tis almost fairy time.

> Shakespeare
> *A Midsummer-Night's Dream*, act V, sc.
> i, l. 372

The kiss you take is better than you
   give.

> Shakespeare
> *Troilus and Cressida*, act IV, sc. v, l. 38

Then, let thy love be younger than
   thyself,
Or thy affection cannot hold the
   bent;
For women are as roses, whose fair
   flower
Being once display'd, doth fall that
   very hour.

> Shakespeare
> *Twelfth-Night*, act II, sc. iv, l. 36

This bud of love, by summer's ripening breath,
May prove a beauteous flower when next we meet.

Shakespeare
Ibid. sc. ii, l. 121

This word "love," which greybeards call divine.

Shakespeare
King Henry the Sixth, Part III, act V, sc. vi, l. 81

Therefore love moderately; long love doth so;
Too swift arrives as tardy as too slow.

Shakespeare
Romeo and Juliet, act II, sc. vi, l. 14

This is the very ecstasy of love.

Shakespeare
Hamlet, act II, sc. i, l. 102

Jaques: What stature is she of?
Orlando: Just as high as my heart.

Shakespeare
As You Like It, act III, sc. ii, l. 286

A woman would run through fire
and water for such a kind heart.

Shakespeare
The Merry Wives of Windsor, act III,
sc. iv, l. 106

All lovers swear more performance
than they are able, and yet re-
serve an ability that they never
perform; vowing more than the
perfection of ten and discharging
less than the tenth part of one.

Shakespeare
Troilus and Cressida, act III, sc. ii, l. 89

Bait the hook well: this fish will
bite.

Shakespeare
Much Ado About Nothing, act II, sc. iii,
l. 121

Base men being in love have then a
nobility in their natures more
than is native to them.

Shakespeare
Othello, act II, sc. i, l. 218

By heaven, I do love, and it hath
taught me to rime, and to be mel-
ancholy.

Shakespeare
Love's Labour's Lost, act IV, sc. iii, l. 13

If the rascal have not given me
medicines to make me love him,
I'll be hanged.

Shakespeare
King Henry the Fourth, Part II, act II,
sc. ii, l. 20

No sooner met, but they looked; no
sooner looked but they loved;
no sooner loved but they sighed;
no sooner sighed but they asked
one another the reason; no sooner
knew the reason but they sought
the remedy.

Shakespeare
As You Like It, act V, sc. ii, l. 37

Speak low, if you speak love.

Shakespeare
Much Ado About Nothing, act II, sc. i,
l. 104

We that are true lovers run into
strange capers.

Shakespeare
As You Like It, act II, sc. iv, l. 53

Down on your knees,
And thank heaven, fasting, for a good
man's love.

Shakespeare
As You Like It, act III, sc. v, l. 57

For aught that I could ever
read,
Could ever hear by tale or history,
The course of true love never did run
smooth.

Shakespeare
A Midsummer-Night's Dream, act I,
sc. i, l. 132

For several virtues
Have I lik'd several women.

Shakespeare
The Tempest, act III, sc. i, l. 42

If ever thou shalt love,
In the sweet pangs of it remember
 me;
For such as I am all true lovers are:
Unstaid and skittish in all motions
 else
Save in the constant image of the
 creature
That is belov'd.

Shakespeare
Twelfth-Night, act II, sc. iv, l. 15

My love's
More richer than my tongue.

Shakespeare
King Lear, act I, sc. i, l. 79

The wounds invisible
That love's keen arrows make.

Shakespeare
As You Like It, act III, sc. v, l. 30

The fickleness of the women I love
is only equaled by the infernal
constancy of the women who love
me.

> George Bernard Shaw
> *The Philanderer* [1893], act II

The test of a man or woman's
breeding is how they behave in a
quarrel.

> Shaw
> Ibid. act IV

And when I feigned an angry look,
Alas! I loved you best.

> John Sheffield, Duke of Buckingham
> and Normanby
> *The Reconcilement* [1701]

I arise from dreams of thee
In the first sweet sleep of night,
When the winds are breathing low,
And the stars are shining bright.

> Percy Bysshe Shelley
> "The Indian Serenade" [1819], st. 1

Through all the drama — whether
damned or not —
Love gilds the scene, and women
guide the plot.

> Richard Brinsley Sheridan
> *The Rivals* [1775]. Epilogue

I loved him for himself alone.

> Sheridan
> *The Duenna* [1775], act I, sc. iii

Have I caught my heav'nly jewel.

> Sir Philip Sidney
> *Astrophel and Stella* [1591]. Second
> song

My true-love hath my heart, and I
have his,
By just exchange one for the other
given:
I hold his dear, and mine he cannot
miss,
There never was a better bargain
driven.

> Sidney
> *The Arcadia* [written 1580]. Sonnet

Ah! when will this long weary day
   have end,
And lend me leave to come unto my
   love?

    Edmund Spenser
    "Epithalamion" [1595], l. 278

Gather therefore the Rose, whilst
   yet is prime,
For soon comes age, that will her
   pride deflower:
Gather the Rose of love, whilst yet is
   time.

    Spenser
    The Faerie Queene [1590], bk. II, canto
    12, st. 75

           Her angel's face
As the great eye of heaven shined
   bright,
And made a sunshine in the shady
   place.

    Spenser
    Ibid. bk. I, canto 3, st. 4

Love is the whole history of a woman's life, it is but an episode in a
   man's.

    Germaine de Staël
    De l'Influence des passions [1796]

Though her mien carries much
   more invitation than command,
   to behold her is an immediate
   check to loose behavior; and to
   love her is a liberal education.

   Sir Richard Steele
   Tatler [1709–1711], no. 49

That old sweetheart of mine.

   James Whitcomb Riley
   "An Old Sweetheart of Mine," st. 12

Out upon it, I have loved
Three whole days together;
And am like to love three more,
If it prove fair weather.

   Sir John Suckling
   Fragmenta Aurea [1646]. A Poem with
      the Answer, st. 1

Why so pale and wan, fond lover?
Prithee, why so pale?
Will, when looking well can't move
   her,
Looking ill prevail?

   Suckling
   Aglaura [1638]. Song, st. 1

Lord, I wonder what fool it was that
first invented kissing!

> Jonathan Swift
> *Polite Conversation* [1738], dialogue 2

If love were what the rose is,
And I were like the leaf,
Our lives would grow together
In sad or singing weather.

> Algernon Charles Swinburne
> "A Match" [1866], st. 1

If you were April's lady,
And I were lord in May.

> Swinburne
> Ibid. st. 5

If you were queen of pleasure,
And I were king of pain,
We'd hunt down love together,
Pluck out his flying feather,
And teach his feet a measure,
And find his mouth a rein.

> Swinburne
> Ibid. st. 6

Lo, this is she that was the world's delight.

> Swinburne
> "Laus Veneris" [1866], st. 3

And I would have, now love is over,
An end to all, an end:
I cannot, having been your lover,
Stoop to become your friend!

> Arthur Symons
> "After Love" [1892], st. 3

'Tis better to have loved and lost
Than never to have loved at all.

> Alfred, Lord Tennyson
> *In Memoriam* [1850], 27, st. 4

And o'er the hills and far away
Beyond their utmost purple rim,
Beyond the night, across the day,
Through all the world she followed
   him.

> Tennyson
> *The Day Dream* [1842]. The Departure,
>   st. 4

He will hold thee, when his passion
   shall have spent its novel force,
Something better than his dog, a
   little dearer than his horse.

> Tennyson
> *Locksley Hall* [1842], l. 49

In the spring a young man's fancy
   lightly turns to thoughts of love.

> Tennyson
> Ibid. l. 20

Now lies the Earth all Danaë to the
   stars,
And all thy heart lies open unto me.

> Tennyson
> *The Princess* [1847], pt. VII. Now
> Sleeps the Crimson Petal, st. 3

She is coming, my own, my sweet;
Were it ever so airy a tread,
My heart would hear her and beat,
Were it earth in an earthy bed;
My dust would hear her and beat,
Had I lain for a century dead;
Would start and tremble under her
   feet,
And blossom in purple and red.

> Tennyson
> *Maud* [1855], pt. I, sec. xxii, st. 11

Lovers' quarrels are the renewal of
love.

> Terence
> *Andria* (*The Lady of Andros*), l.555

Love is swift, sincere, pious, pleasant, gentle, strong, patient, faithful, prudent, long-suffering,
manly and never seeking her own;
for wheresoever a man seeketh
his own, there he falleth from
love.

> Thomas à Kempis
> *Imitation of Christ* [c. 1420], bk. III, 5

Such a one do I remember, whom
to look at was to love.

> Tennyson
> *Locksley Hall*, l. 72

'Tis strange what a man may do,
and a woman yet think him an
angel.

> William Makepeace Thackeray
> *Henry Esmond* [1852], bk. I, ch. 7

Here are fruits, flowers, leaves and
  branches,
And here is my heart which beats
  only for you.

> Paul Verlaine
> *Romances sans Paroles* [1874], Green

I feel again a spark of that ancient
  flame.

> Virgil
> *Aeneid*, bk. IV, l. 23

Who does not love wine, women,
  and song
Remains a fool his whole life long.

> Johann Heinrich Voss
> Attributed

Yes, I'm in love, I feel it now
And Caelia has undone me;
And yet I swear I can't tell how
The pleasing plague stole on me.

> William Whitehead
> "The Je ne sçay quoi song"

I am she who adorn'd herself and
   folded her hair expectantly,
My truant lover has come, and it is
   dark.

> Walt Whitman
> *Leaves of Grass* [1891–1892]. The
> Sleepers, 1

I have found it impossible to carry
   the heavy burden of responsibility
   and to discharge my duties as
   King as I would wish to do without the help and support of the
   woman I love.

> Edward, Duke of Windsor
> Farewell broadcast after abdication
>   [December 11, 1936]

She was a phantom of delight
When first she gleamed upon my
   sight;
A lovely apparition, sent
To be a moment's ornament.

> William Wordsworth
> "She Was a Phantom of Delight"
>   [1807], st. 1

Love lodged in a woman's breast
Is but a guest.

> Sir Henry Wotton
> "A Woman's Heart" [1651]

And many a poor man that has
   roved,
Loved and thought himself beloved,
From a glad kindness cannot take his
   eyes.

     William Butler Yeats
     Michael Robartes and the Dancer
       [1921]. A Prayer for My Daughter,
       st. 5

But is there any comfort to be
   found?
Man is in love and loves what van-
   ishes,
What more is there to say?

     Yeats
     The Tower [1928]. Nineteen Hundred
       and Nineteen, I, st. 6

Down by the salley gardens my love
   and I did meet;
She passed the salley gardens with
   little snow-white feet.
She bid me take love easy, as the
   leaves grow on the tree;
But I, being young and foolish, with
   her would not agree.

     Yeats
     Crossways [1889]. Down by the Salley
       Gardens

How many loved your moments of
    glad grace,
And loved your beauty with love false
    or true,
But one man loved the pilgrim soul in
    you,
And loved the sorrows of your chang-
    ing face.

> Yeats
> *The Rose* [1893]. When You Are Old,
>   st. 2

I gave what other women gave
That stepped out of their clothes,
But when this soul, its body off,
Naked to naked goes,
He it has found shall find therein
What none other knows.

> Yeats
> *The Winding Stair and Other Poems*
>   [1933]. A Woman Young and Old,
>   IX, A Last Confession, st. 3

I had wild Jack for a lover.

> Yeats
> Ibid. Words for Music Perhaps, V,
>   Crazy Jane on God, st. 4

Never give all the heart, for love
Will hardly seem worth thinking of
To passionate women if it seem
Certain, and they never dream
That it fades out from kiss to kiss;
For everything that's lovely is
But a brief, dreamy kind delight.

  Yeats
  In the Seven Woods [1904]. Never Give
  All the Heart

In courtesy I'd have her chiefly
  learned;
Hearts are not had as a gift but hearts
  are earned.

  Yeats
  Michael Robartes and the Dancer.
  A Prayer for My Daughter, st. 5

No man has ever lived that had
  enough
Of children's gratitude or woman's
  love.

  Yeats
  The Winding Stair and Other Poems.
  Vacillation, III, st. 1

Speech after long silence; it is right,
All other lovers being estranged or
  dead . . .
That we descant and yet again des-
  cant
Upon the supreme theme of Art and
  Song:
Bodily decrepitude is wisdom; young
We loved each other and were igno-
  rant.

> Yeats
> Ibid. XVII, After Long Silence

Unwearied still, lover by lover,
They paddle in the cold
Companionable streams or climb the
  air;
Their hearts have not grown old.

> Yeats
> *The Wild Swans at Coole* [1919]. The
> Wild Swans at Coole, st. 4

Lie to me. Tell me all these years
  you've waited. Tell me.

> Philip Yordan
> *Johnny Guitar* (screenplay) [1954]

Passion

At best, the renewal of broken relations is a nervous matter.

> Henry Adams
> *The Education of Henry Adams* [1907],
> ch. 16

All lovely things will have an ending,
All lovely things will fade and die,
And youth, that's now so bravely spending,
Will beg a penny by and by.

> Conrad Aiken
> "All Lovely Things"

Who loves a garden still his Eden keeps,
Perennial pleasures plants, and wholesome harvests reaps.

> Bronson Alcott
> *Tablets* [1868]

Love me little, love me long,
Is the burden of my song.

> Anonymous
> "Love Me Little" [1569–1570], refrain

A fool's paradise.

> Anonymous
> *Paston Letters* [1462], no 457

Gaudeamus igitur,
Iuvenes dum sumus.
[Let us live then and be glad
While young life is before us.]

> Anonymous Latin
> Students' song [c. 1267]

O Western wind, when wilt thou
  blow
That the small rain down can rain?
Christ, that my love were in my arms
And I in my bed again!

> Anonymous [c. 1530]

Eternal passion!
Eternal pain!

> Matthew Arnold
> "Philomela" [1853], st. 3

Thou hast no *right* to bliss.

> Arnold
> *Empedocles on Etna* [1852], act I, sc. ii,
>   l. 160

We cannot kindle when we will
The fire that in the heart resides,
The spirit bloweth and is still,
In mystery our soul abides.

> Arnold
> "Morality" [1852], st. 1

Greatness is a spiritual condition
   worthy to excite love, interest,
   and admiration.

> Arnold
> *Culture and Anarchy* [1869].
>   Sweetness and Light

Like love we don't know where or
   why
Like love we can't compel or fly
Like love we often weep
Like love we seldom keep.

> W. H. Auden
> "Law Like Love" [1940], last stanza

The dove loves when it quarrels; the
wolf hates when it flatters.

> Saint Augustine
> Sermones, 64

Our heart is a treasury; if you spend
all its wealth at once you are ru-
ined. We find it as difficult to
forgive a person for displaying his
feeling in all its nakedness as we
do to forgive a man for being pen-
niless.

> Honoré de Balzac
> *Le Père Goriot* [1835]

Tell me the tales that to me were so
dear,
Long, long ago, long, long ago.

> Thomas Haynes Bayly
> "Long, Long Ago"

Call no man foe, but never love a
stranger.

> Stella Benson
> "To the Unborn," st. 3

Hell, Madame, is to love no longer.

Georges Bernanos
Le Journal d'un curé de campagne
(The Diary of a Country Priest)

Hatred stirreth up strifes: but love
covereth all sins.

The Bible
Old Testament
Proverbs 10:12

I am my beloved's, and his desire is
toward me.

Old Testament
The Song of Solomon 7:10

I drew them with . . . bands of love.

Old Testament
Hosea 11:4

My soul thirsteth for thee, my flesh
longeth for thee in a dry and
thirsty land, where no water is.

> Old Testament
> Psalms 63:1

Many waters cannot quench love,
neither can the floods drown it.

> Old Testament
> The Song of Solomon 8:7

I shall light a candle of understanding in thine heart, which shall not
be put out.

> Apocrypha
> II Esdras 14:25

Her sins, which are many, are for-
given; for she loved much.

> New Testament
> Luke 7:47

For Mercy has a human heart,
Pity, a human face,
And Love, the human form divine,
And Peace, the human dress.

> William Blake
> *Songs of Innocence* [1789–1790].
>   The Divine Image, st. 3

— O remember
In your narrowing dark hours
That more things move
Than blood in the heart.

> Louise Bogan
> "Night," st. 4

They love him most for the enemies
   he has made.

> Edward S. Bragg
> Speech seconding the presidential
>   nomination of Grover Cleveland
>   [July 9, 1884]

Keep your sunny side up.

> Lew Brown and Buddy De Sylva
> *Sunny Side Up* [1929], title song

"Guess now who holds thee?" —
    "Death," I said. But there
The silver answer rang — "Not
    Death, but Love."

> Elizabeth Barrett Browning
> *Sonnets from the Portuguese* [1850],
>   no. 1

Do I find love so full in my nature,
    God's ultimate gift,
That I doubt his own love can com-
    pete with it? Here, the parts shift?

> Robert Browning
> "Saul" [1855], st. 17

How good is man's life, the mere
    living! how fit to employ
All the heart and the soul and the
    senses forever in joy!

> Browning
> Ibid. st. 9

Let's contend no more, Love,
Strive nor weep:
All be as before, Love,
— Only sleep!

> Browning
> "A Woman's Last Word" [1855], st. 1

Never the time and the place
And the loved one all together!

> Browning
> "Never the Time and the Place" [1883]

Oh heart! oh blood that freezes,
    blood that burns!
        Earth's returns
For whole centuries of folly, noise
    and sin!
        Shut them in,
With their triumphs and their glories
    and the rest!
        Love is best!

> Browning
> "Love Among the Ruins" [1855], st. 7

Such ever was love's way: to rise, it
stoops.

> Browning
> "A Death in the Desert" [1864], l. 134

Thou shalt love and be loved by,
    forever: a Hand like this hand
Shall throw open the gates of new life
    to thee! See the Christ stand!

> Browning
> "Saul," st. 18

To him who in the love of Nature
  holds
Communion with her visible forms,
  she speaks
A various language.

> William Cullen Bryant
> *Thanatopsis* [1817–1821], l. 1

Love, like Death,
Levels all ranks, and lays the shep-
  herd's crook
Beside the scepter.

> Edward Bulwer-Lytton
> *The Lady of Lyons* [1838], act III, sc. ii

I am Tarzan of the Apes. I want
  you. I am yours. You are mine.

> Edgar Rice Burroughs
> *Tarzan of the Apes* [1914], ch. 18

No cord nor cable can so forcibly
  draw, or hold so fast, as love can
  do with a twined thread.

> Robert Burton
> *The Anatomy of Melancholy* [1621–
>   1651], pt. III, sec. 2, member 1,
>   subsec. 2

To enlarge or illustrate this power
and effect of love is to set a candle in the sun.

> Burton
> Ibid.

God is Love — I dare say. But what
a mischievous devil Love is!

> Samuel Butler
> *Notebooks* [1912]. God Is Love

The isles of Greece, the isles of
Greece!
Where burning Sappho loved and
sung.

> Lord Byron
> *Don Juan*, canto III [1821], st. 86
> [song, st. 1]

A little still she strove, and much
repented,
And whispering, "I will ne'er con-
sent" — consented.

> Lord Byron
> Ibid. canto I [1818], st. 117

Follow your bliss.

> Joseph Campbell
> *The Power of Myth* [1988]

The summer hath his joys,
And winter his delights;
Though love and all his pleasures are
　　but toys,
They shorten tedious nights.

> Thomas Campion
> *Third Book of Airs* [1617]. XII

I've looked on a lot of women with
　　lust. I've committed adultery in
　　my heart many times. This is
　　something that God recognizes I
　　will do — and I have done it —
　　and God forgives me for it.

> Jimmy Carter
> Interview in *Playboy* magazine
> [October 1976]

That is happiness; to be dissolved
　　into something complete and
　　great.

> Willa Cather
> *My Ántonia* [1918], bk. I, ch. 2

Body, remember not only how
    much you were loved,
not only the beds you lay on,
but also those desires glowing openly
in eyes that looked at you,
trembling for you in voices.

> C. P. Cavafy
> "Body, Remember" [1918]

If you love, you will suffer, and if
    you do not love, you do not know
    the meaning of a Christian life.

> Agatha Christie
> *An Autobiography* [1977], Pt. III.
> Growing Up

All thoughts, all passions, all de-
    lights,
Whatever stirs this mortal frame,
All are but ministers of Love,
And feed his sacred flame.

> Samuel Taylor Coleridge
> "Love" [1799], st. 1

"I haven't much time to be fond of anything," says Sergeant Cuff. "But when I *have* a moment's fondness to bestow, most times . . . the roses get it."

Wilkie Collins
The Moonstone [1868]. First Period, ch. 12

Love our principle, order our foundation, progress our goal.

Auguste Comte
Système de politique positive [1851–1854]

My love was so hot as mighty nigh to burst my boilers.

David Crockett
Narrative of the Life of Colonel Crockett [1834]

A great flame follows a little spark.

> Dante Alighieri
> *The Divine Comedy* [c. 1310–1321].
>   Paradiso, canto I, l. 34

Love kindled by virtue always kindles another, provided that its flame appear outwardly.

> Dante
> Ibid. Purgatorio, canto XXII, l. 10

There is a passion for hunting something deeply implanted in the human breast.

> Charles Dickens
> *Oliver Twist* [1837–1838], ch. 10

Love — is anterior to Life —
Posterior — to Death —
Initial of Creation, and
The Exponent of Earth.

Emily Dickinson
No. 917 [c. 1864]

That it will never come again
Is what makes life so sweet.

Dickinson
No. 1741 [n.d.], st. 1

All Kings, and all their favorites,
All glory of honors, beauties, wits,
The sun itself, which makes times, as
   they pass,
Is elder by a year, now, than it was
When thou and I first one another
   saw:
All other things, to their destruction
   draw,
Only our love hath no decay;
This, no tomorrow hath, nor yester-
   day,
Running, it never runs from us away,
But truly keeps his first, last, everlast-
   ing day.

John Donne
"The Anniversary," st. 1

And now good morrow to our wak-
  ing souls,
Which watch not one another out of
  fear;
For love, all love of other sights con-
  trols,
And makes one little room, an everywhere.
Let sea-discoverers to new worlds
  have gone,
Let maps to other, worlds on worlds
  have shown,
Let us possess one world, each hath
  one, and is one.

> Donne
> "The Good Morrow," st. 2

For God sake hold your tongue, and
  let me love.

> Donne
> "The Canonization," st. 1

Love, all alike, no season knows,
  nor clime,
Nor hours, days, months, which are
  the rags of time.

> Donne
> "The Sun Rising," st. 1

Full nakedness! All joys are due to
   thee,
As souls unbodied, bodies unclothed
   must be,
To taste whole joys.

> Donne
> "To His Mistress Going to Bed," l. 24

To rage, to lust, to write to, to com-
   mend,
All is the purlieu of the god of love.

> Donne
> "Love's Deity," st. 3

Come on, baby, light my fire
Try to set the night on fire.

> The Doors
> "Light My Fire" [1967]

Man is sometimes extraordinarily,
   passionately, in love with suffering.

> Fëdor Dostoevski
> *Notes from the Underground* [1864],
>   ch. 9

I am the Love that dare not speak
its name.

> Lord Alfred Douglas
> "Two Loves" [1894]

They are not long, the weeping and
the laughter,
Love and desire and hate:
I think they have no portion in us
after
We pass the gate.

They are not long, the days of wine
and roses;
Out of a misty dream
Our path emerges for a while, then
closes
Within a dream.

> Ernest Dowson
> "Vitae Summa Brevis Spem Nos Vetat
> Incohare Longam" [1896]

In your rocking chair by your window shall you dream such happiness as you may never feel.

> Theodore Dreiser
> *Sister Carrie* [1900], 50

Our chief want in life is somebody
who shall make us do what we
can.

> Ralph Waldo Emerson
> *The Conduct of Life* [1860]. Consider-
> ations by the Way

When I write of hunger, I am really
writing about love and the hunger
for it, and warmth and the love of
it and the hunger for it . . . and
then the warmth and richness
and fine reality of hunger satisfied
. . . and it is all one.

> M. F. K. Fisher
> *The Gastronomical Me* [1943].
> Foreword

Ah Love! could you and I with Him
conspire
To grasp this Sorry Scheme of Things
entire,
Would not we shatter it to bits —
and then
Remold it nearer to the Heart's Desire!

> Edward FitzGerald
> *The Rubáiyát of Omar Khayyám* [1879],
> st. 99

For some we loved, the loveliest
  and the best
That from his Vintage rolling Time
  hath prest.

> FitzGerald
> Ibid. st. 22

One must not always think that
  feeling is everything. Art is nothing without form.

> Gustave Flaubert
> Letter to Madame Louise Colet
>   [August 12, 1846]

She [Madame Bovary] had that in-
  definable beauty that comes from
  happiness, enthusiasm, success — a beauty that is nothing
  more or less than a harmony of
  temperament and circumstances.

> Flaubert
> *Madame Bovary* [1857], pt. II, ch. 12

There isn't a bourgeois alive who in the ferment of his youth, if only for a day or for a minute, hasn't thought himself capable of boundless passions and noble exploits. The sorriest little woman-chaser has dreamed of Oriental queens; in a corner of every notary's heart lie the moldy remains of a poet.

> Flaubert
> Ibid. pt. III, ch. 6

A tale without love is like beef without mustard: insipid.

> Anatole France
> *The Revolt of the Angels* [1914], ch. 8

Beautiful dreamer, wake unto me, Starlight and dewdrop are waiting for thee.

> Stephen Foster
> "Beautiful Dreamer" [1864], st. 1

Dost thou love life? Then do not squander time; for that's the stuff life is made of.

> Benjamin Franklin
> *Poor Richard's Almanac* [1746]. June

Singin' in the rain, just singin' in the
  rain.
What a glorious feeling, I'm happy
  again.

> Arthur Freed
> "Singin' in the Rain" [1929]

Man's nature, his passions and anxi-
  eties, are a cultural product; as a
  matter of fact, man himself is the
  most important creation and
  achievement of the continuous
  human effort, the record of what
  we call history.

> Erich Fromm
> *Escape from Freedom* [1941], ch. 1

Fill ev'ry glass, for wine inspires us,
And fires us
With courage, love and joy.
Women and wine should life employ.
Is there ought else on earth desirous?

> John Gay
> *The Beggar's Opera* [1728], act II, sc. i,
> air 19

Youth's the season made for joys,
Love is then our duty.

> Gay
> Ibid. sc. iv, air 22

I saw and loved.

> Edward Gibbon
> *Memoirs (Autobiography)* [1796]

I love those who yearn for the impossible.

> Johann Wolfgang von Goethe
> *Faust* [1808–1832]. The Second Part,
> Classical Walpurgis Night

Pleasure and love are the pinions of great deeds.

> Goethe
> *Iphigenia in Tauris* [1787], act II, sc. i

A little season of love and laughter,
Of light and life, and pleasure and pain,
And a horror of outer darkness after,
And dust returneth to dust again.

> Adam Lindsay Gordon
> "The Swimmer"

Aesthetic emotion puts man in a
state favorable to the reception of
erotic emotion. Art is the accom-
plice of love. Take love away and
there is no longer art.

> Remy de Gourmont
> Décadence

As you are woman, so be lovely:
As you are lovely, so be various,
Merciful as constant, constant as
various,
So be mine, as I yours for ever.

> Robert Graves
> "Pygmalion to Galatea"

When love could teach a monarch
to be wise,
And gospel-light first dawn'd from
Bullen's eyes.

> Thomas Gray
> *The Alliance of Education and Govern-*
> *ment* [c. 1748], 1. 108

You're only here for a short visit.
Don't hurry. Don't worry. And be
sure to smell the flowers along
the way.

> Walter C. Hagen
> *The Walter Hagen Story* [1956]

Oh, what a beautiful mornin'
Oh, what a beautiful day.
I got a beautiful feelin'
Everything's going my way.

> Oscar Hammerstein II
> *Oklahoma!* [1943]. Oh, What a Beautiful Mornin'

Let men tremble to win the hand of woman, unless they win along with it the utmost passion of her heart.

> Nathaniel Hawthorne
> *The Scarlet Letter* [1850], ch. 15

The love of liberty is the love of others; the love of power is the love of ourselves.

> William Hazlitt
> *Political Essays*. The *Times* Newspaper

We may affirm absolutely that nothing great in the world has been accomplished without passion.

> Georg Wilhelm Friedrich Hegel
> *Philosophy of History* [1832]. Introduction

But did thee feel the earth move?

> Ernest Hemingway
> *For Whom the Bell Tolls* [1940], ch. 13

Love bade me welcome: yet my soul
    drew back,
Guilty of dust and sin.
But quick-ey'd Love, observing me
    grow slack
From my first entrance in,
Drew nearer to me, sweetly question-
    ing,
If I lack'd anything.

> George Herbert
> *The Temple* [1633]. Love, st. 1

You must sit down, says Love, and
    taste my meat:
So I did sit and eat.

> Herbert
> Ibid. st. 3

Love, who is most beautiful among
    the immortal gods, the melter of
    limbs, overwhelms in their hearts
    the intelligence and wise counsel
    of all gods and all men.

> Hesiod
> *The Theogony*, l. 120

Observe due measure, for right timing is in all things the most important factor.

> Hesiod
> *Works and Days*, l.694

There is a fullness of all things, even of sleep and of love.

> Homer
> *The Iliad*, bk. XIII, l. 636

Our common lust for life.

> Henrik Ibsen
> *Hedda Gabler* [1890], act II

Life is an end in itself, and the only question as to whether it is worth living is whether you have enough of it.

> Oliver Wendell Holmes, Jr.
> Speech at Bar Association Dinner,
> Boston [1900]

Beauty is in the eye of the beholder.

> Margaret Wolfe Hungerford
> *Molly Bawn* [1878]

You can't always get what you want
But if you try sometimes
You just might find
You get what you need.

> Mick Jagger and Keith Richards
> "You Can't Always Get What You
> Want" [1969]

Be not afraid of life. Believe that
life *is* worth living, and your belief
will help create the fact.

> William James
> *The Will to Believe* [1897]. Is Life
> Worth Living?

There is but one unconditional
commandment, which is that we
should seek incessantly, with fear
and trembling, so to vote and to
act as to bring about the very larg-
est total universe of good which
we can see.

> James
> Ibid. The Moral Philosopher and the
> Moral Life

This life is worth living, we can say,
since it is what we make it, from
the moral point of view.

> James
> Ibid. Is Life Worth Living?

Does it matter whether you hate
     your . . . self?
          At least
Love your eyes that can see, your
     mind that can
Hear the music, the thunder of the
     wings. Love the wild swan.

> Robinson Jeffers
> "Love the Wild Swan"

When angry, count ten before you
     speak; if very angry, an hundred.

> Thomas Jefferson
> *A Decalogue of Canons for Observation
> in Practical Life* [February 21, 1825]

Love knows nothing of order.

> Saint Jerome
> Letter 7

The joy of life is variety; the tender-
     est love requires to be rekindled
     by intervals of absence.

> Samuel Johnson
> *The Idler* [1758–1760], no. 39

There shall be no love lost.

> Ben Jonson
> *Every Man out of His Humour* [1599],
> act II, sc. i

I thought well as well him as another and then I asked him with
   my eyes to ask again yes and then
   he asked me would I yes to say
   yes my mountain flower and first
   I put my arms around him yes
   and drew him down to me so he
   could feel my breasts all perfume
   yes and his heart was going like
   mad and yes I said yes I will Yes.

> James Joyce
> *Ulysses* [1922]. Last words

How simple and frugal a thing is
   happiness: a glass of wine, a roast
   chestnut, a wretched little bra-
   zier, the sound of the sea. . . . All
   that is required to feel that here
   and now is happiness is a simple,
   frugal heart.

> Nikos Kazantzakis
> *Zorba the Greek* [1946], ch. 7

When I behold, upon the night's
  starr'd face,
Huge cloudy symbols of a high romance.

> John Keats
> *Life, Letters, and Literary Remains of
> John Keats*, ed. Richard Monckton
> Milnes [1848]. Sonnet. When I Have
> Fears

I am certain of nothing but of the
  holiness of the Heart's affections
  and the truth of Imagination —
  What the imagination seizes as
  Beauty must be truth — whether
  it existed before or not.

> Keats
> Letter to Benjamin Bailey [November
> 22, 1817]

O for a Life of Sensations rather
  than of Thoughts!

> Keats
> Ibid.

Hot and bothered.

> Rudyard Kipling
> "Independence." Rectorial Address at
> St. Andrews [October 10, 1923]

Thou truly canst not guide whom
thou lovest; but God guideth
whom He will; and He best
knoweth those who yield to guid-
ance.

> The Koran
> Chapter 28:55

O time, arrest your flight! and you,
propitious hours, arrest your
course! Let us savor the fleeting
delights of our most beautiful
days!

> Alphonse de Lamartine
> "The Lake" [1820], st. 6

I love to lose myself in other men's
minds.

> Charles Lamb
> *Last Essays of Elia* [1833]. Detached
> Thoughts on Books and Reading

It is good to love the unknown.

> Lamb
> *Essays of Elia* [1823]. Valentine's Day

I have three treasures. Guard and
  keep them:
  The first is deep love,
  The second is frugality,
  And the third is not to dare to be
  ahead of the world.
Because of deep love, one is coura-
  geous.
Because of frugality, one is generous.
Because of not daring to be ahead of
  the world, one becomes the leader
  of the world.

>   Lao-tzu
>   *The Way of Lao-Tzu* 67

Self-love is the greatest of all flatter-
ers.

>   François, Duc de La Rochefoucauld
>   *Reflections; or, Sentences and Moral
>   Maxims* [1678], maxim 2

The pleasure of love is in loving.
  We are happier in the passion we
  feel than in that we arouse.

>   La Rochefoucauld
>   Ibid. maxim 259

For man, as for flower and beast
and bird, the supreme triumph is
to be most vividly, most perfectly
alive.

D. H. Lawrence
Apocalypse [1931]

The Owl and the Pussycat went to
sea
In a beautiful pea-green boat,
They took some honey, and plenty of
money,
Wrapped up in a five-pound note.
The Owl looked up to the stars above,
And sang to a small guitar,
"O lovely Pussy! O Pussy, my love,
What a beautiful Pussy you are."
Pussy said to the Owl, "You elegant
fowl!
How charmingly sweet you sing!
O let us be married! too long we have
tarried:
But what shall we do for a ring?"
They sailed away, for a year and a day,
To the land where the Bong-tree
grows
And there in a wood a Piggy-wig
stood
With a ring at the end of his nose.

Edward Lear
"The Owl and the Pussycat" [1871],
st. 1–2

Don't let it be forgot
That once there was a spot
For one brief shining moment that
    was known
As Camelot.

> Alan Jay Lerner
> *Camelot* [1960], end

There was never any yet that wholly
    could escape love, and never shall
    there be any, never so long as
    beauty shall be, never so long as
    eyes can see.

> Longus
> *Daphnis and Chloe*, proem, ch. 2

Stone walls do not a prison make,
Nor iron bars a cage;
Minds innocent and quiet take
That for an hermitage;
If I have freedom in my love,
And in my soul am free,
Angels alone that soar above
Enjoy such liberty.

> Richard Lovelace
> *Lucasta* [1649]. To Althea: From
>   Prison, st. 4

Every man feels instinctively that all the beautiful sentiments in the world weigh less than a single lovely action.

> James Russell Lowell
> *Literary Essays*, vol. II [1870–1890].
> New England Two Centuries Ago

For thee the wonder-working earth puts forth sweet flowers.

> Lucretius
> *De Rerum Natura* (On the Nature of Things), bk. I, l. 7

There is no feeling in a human heart which exists in that heart alone — which is not, in some form or degree, in every heart.

> George Macdonald
> *Unspoken Sermons*, second series [1885]

The month of May was come, when
every lusty heart beginneth to
blossom, and to bring forth fruit;
for like as herbs and trees bring
forth fruit and flourish in May, in
likewise every lusty heart that is
in any manner a lover, springeth
and flourisheth in lusty deeds.
For it giveth unto all lovers courage, that lusty month of May.

Sir Thomas Malory
Le Morte d'Arthur [1485], bk. XVIII,
ch. 25

Mankind is composed of two sorts
of men — those who love and
create, and those who hate and
destroy.

José Martí
Letter to a Cuban farmer [1893]

I would
Love you ten years before the Flood,
And you should, if you please, refuse
Till the conversion of the Jews.
My vegetable love should grow
Vaster than empires, and more slow.

Andrew Marvell
"To His Coy Mistress" [1650–1652]

The tragedy of love is indifference.

W. Somerset Maugham
The Trembling of a Leaf [1921], ch. 4

At times discretion should be
thrown aside, and with the foolish
we should play the fool.

Menander
Those Offered for Sale, fragment 421

For singing till his heaven fills,
'Tis love of earth that he instills,
And ever winging up and up,
Our valley is his golden cup,
And he the wine which over flows
To lift us with him as he goes.

George Meredith
"The Lark Ascending" [1881], l. 65

Instill the love of you into all the
world, for a good character is
what is remembered.

The Teaching for Merikare, par. 24

I live and love in God's peculiar
light.

Michelangelo
Sonnet

It's good to be just plain happy; it's a little better to know that you're happy; but to understand that you're happy and to know why and how . . . and still be happy, be happy in the being and the knowing, well that is beyond happiness, that is bliss.

> Henry Miller
> *The Colossus of Maroussi* [1941], pt. I

See golden days, fruitful of golden deeds,
With Joy and Love triumphing.

> John Milton
> *Paradise Lost* [1667], bk. III, l. 337

The evening star,
Love's harbinger.

> Milton
> Ibid. bk. XI, l. 588

Paradise itself were dim
And joyless, if not shared with him!

> Thomas Moore
> *Lalla Rookh* [1817], pt. VI

Do Not Trifle with Love.

Alfred de Musset
Title of a comedy [1834]

Goodness, armed with power, is corrupted; and pure love without power is destroyed.

Reinhold Niebuhr
Beyond Tragedy [1938]

Love is enough, though the world be awaning.

William Morris
"Love is Enough" [1872]

Lolita, light of my life, fire of my loins. My sin, my soul.

Vladimir Nabokov
Lolita [1955], pt. I, ch. 1

Nothing worth doing is completed in our lifetime; therefore, we must be saved by hope. Nothing true or beautiful or good makes complete sense in any immediate context of history; therefore, we must be saved by faith. Nothing we do, however, virtuous, can be accomplished alone; therefore, we are saved by love.

Niebuhr
The Irony of American History [1952]

Love is the state in which man sees things most widely different from what they are. The force of illusion reaches its zenith here, as likewise the sweetening and transfiguring power. When a man is in love he endures more than at other times; he submits to everything.

Friedrich Nietzsche
The Antichrist [1888], aphorism 23

Dreams are necessary to life.

Anaïs Nin
The Diary of Anaïs Nin, vol. II [1967], June 1936 (letter to her mother)

Desire Under the Elms.

> Eugene O'Neill
> Title of play [1924]

The red rose whispers of passion
And the white rose breathes of love;
O, the red rose is a falcon,
And the white rose is a dove.

> John Boyle O'Reilly
> "A White Rose," st. 1

Love yields to business. If you seek
a way out of love, be busy; you'll
be safe then.

> Ovid
> *Remedia Amoris*, 143

For hatred does not cease by hatred
at any time: hatred ceases by
love — this is the eternal law.

> The Pali Canon
> Suttapitaka. Dhammapada, ch. 1,
> verse 5

As happy a man as any in the world,
for the whole world seems to
smile upon me.

> Samuel Pepys
> Diary, October 31, 1662

My heart was in my mouth.

Gaius Petronius
Satyricon, sec. 62

And the true order of going, or being led by another, to the things
of love, is to begin from the beauties of earth and mount upwards
for the sake of that other beauty,
using these steps only, and from
one going on to two, and from
two to all fair forms to fair practices, and from fair practices to
fair notions, until from fair notions he arrives at the notion of
absolute beauty, and at last
knows what the essence of beauty
is.

Plato
Dialogues, Symposium, 211

O, human love! thou spirit given,
On Earth, of all we hope in Heaven!

Edgar Allan Poe
Tamerlane [1827], l. 177

Thou wast that all to me, love,
For which my soul did pine —
A green isle in the sea, love,
A fountain and a shrine,
All wreathed with fairy fruits and
  flowers,
And all the flowers were mine.

> Poe
> "To One in Paradise" [1834], st. 1

There is something in the unselfish
  and self-sacrificing love of a
  brute, which goes directly to the
  heart of him who has had fre-
  quent occasion to test the paltry
  friendship and gossamer fidelity
  of mere Man.

> Poe
> "The Black Cat" [1843]

The ruling passion, be it what it
  will,
The ruling passion conquers reason
  still.

> Alexander Pope
> *Moral Essays* [1731–1735]. Epistle III,
> To Lord Bathurst, l. 153

It's delightful, it's delicious, it's de-
lovely.

> Cole Porter
> *Red, Hot and Blue* [1936].
> It's De-Lovely

The time which we have at our dis-
posal every day is elastic; the passions that we feel expand it, those
that we inspire contract it; and
habit fills up what remains.

> Marcel Proust
> *Remembrance of Things Past* [1913–
> 1927]. Within a Budding Grove, pt. 1

Our passions are most like to floods
and streams,
The shallow murmur, but the deep
are dumb.

> Sir Walter Ralegh
> "Sir Walter Ralegh to the Queen"
> [c. 1599], st. 1

The most visible joy can only reveal
itself to us when we've transformed it, within.

> Rainer Maria Rilke
> *Duino Elegies*, 7

Love begets love. This torment is
   my joy.

   Theodore Roethke
   "The Motion" [1964], II

What I love is near at hand,
Always, in earth and air.

   Roethke
   "The Far Field" [1964], III

Live now, believe me, wait not till
   tomorrow;
Gather the roses of life today.

   Pierre de Ronsard
   Sonnets pour Hélène, I, 43

Sweetheart, come see if the rose
Which at morning began to unclose
Its damask gown to the sun
Has not lost, now the day is done,
The folds of its damasked gown
And its colors so like your own.

   Ronsard
   Odes [1553]. À Cassandre

Better by far you should forget and
  smile
Than that you should remember and
  be sad.

> Christina Rossetti
> "Remember" [1862], l. 13

My heart is like a singing bird.

> Rossetti
> "A Birthday" [1861], st. 1

The birthday of my life
Is come, my love is come to me.

> Rossetti
> Ibid. st. 2

Three passions, simple but over-
  whelmingly strong, have governed
  my life: the longing for love, the
  search for knowledge, and un-
  bearable pity for the suffering of
  mankind.

> Bertrand Russell
> *Autobiography* [1967], prologue

It is only with the heart that one
  can see rightly; what is essential
  is invisible to the eye.

> Antoine de Saint-Exupéry
> *The Little Prince* [1943], ch. 21

Faith is an excitement and an enthusiasm: it is a condition of intellectual magnificence to which we must cling as to a treasure, and not squander . . . in the small coin of empty words, or in exact and priggish argument.

> George Sand
> *Letter to Des Planches* [May 25, 1866]

Love, bumping his head blindly against all the obstacles of civilization.

> Sand
> *Indiana* [1832], preface

No human creature can give orders to love.

> Sand
> *Jacques* [1834]

O World, thou choosest not the better part!
It is not wisdom to be only wise,
And on the inward vision close the eyes,
But it is wisdom to believe the heart.

> George Santayana
> "O World, Thou Choosest Not" [1894]

Happiness is the only sanction of
life; where happiness fails, existence remains a mad and lamen-
table experiment.

> Santayana
> *The Life of Reason* [1905–1906], vol. I.
> Reason in Common Sense

In peace, Love tunes the shepherd's
reed;
In war, he mounts the warrior's
steed;
In halls, in gay attire is seen;
In hamlets, dances on the green.
Love rules the court, the camp, the
grove,
And men below, and saints above;
For love is heaven, and heaven is
love.

> Sir Walter Scott
> *The Lay of the Last Minstrel* [1805],
> canto III, st. 2

Phyllis is my only joy,
Faithless as the winds or seas;
Sometimes coming, sometimes coy,
Yet she never fails to please.

> Sir Charles Sedley
> Song [1702], st. 1

Alas, how love can trifle with itself!

William Shakespeare
The Two Gentlemen of Verona, act IV,
sc. iv, l. 190

Doubt thou the stars are fire;
Doubt that the sun doth move;
Doubt truth to be a liar;
But never doubt I love.

Shakespeare
Hamlet, act II, sc. ii, l. 115

I may command where I adore.

Shakespeare
Twelfth-Night, act II, sc. v, l. 116

If music be the food of love, play
    on;
Give me excess of it, that, surfeiting,
The appetite may sicken, and so die.
That strain again! it had a dying fall:
O! it came o'er my ear like the sweet
    sound
That breathes upon a bank of violets,
Stealing and giving odor!

Shakespeare
Ibid. act I, sc. i, l. 1

If you remember'st not the slightest
    folly
That ever love did make thee run
    into,
Thou hast not lov'd.

> Shakespeare
> *As You Like It*, act, II, sc. iv, l. 34

Love is a spirit all compact of fire,
Not gross to sink, but light, and will
    aspire.

> Shakespeare
> *Venus and Adonis*, l. 149

Love thyself last: cherish those
    hearts that hate thee;
Corruption wins not more than hon-
    esty.
Still in thy right hand carry gentle
    peace,
To silence envious tongues: be just,
    and fear not.
Let all the ends thou aim'st at be thy
    country's,
Thy God's, and truth's; then if thou
    fall'st, O Cromwell!
Thou fall'st a blessed martyr!

> Shakespeare
> *King Henry the Eighth*, act III, sc. ii,
> l. 444

O spirit of love! how quick and
  fresh art thou,
That, notwithstanding thy capacity
Receiveth as the sea, nought enters
  there,
Of what validity and pitch soe'er,
But falls into abatement and low
  price,
Even in a minute: so full of shapes is
  fancy,
That it alone is high fantastical.

> Shakespeare
> *Twelfth-Night*, act I, sc. i, l. 9

O! how this spring of love resem-
  bleth
The uncertain glory of an April day!

> Shakespeare
> *The Two Gentlemen of Verona*, act I,
>   sc. iii, l. 84

There's beggary in the love that can
  be reckon'd.

> Shakespeare
> *Antony and Cleopatra*, act I, sc. i, l. 15

Thou last, not least in love.

> Shakespeare
> *Julius Caesar*, act III, sc. i, l. 189

What is love? 'tis not hereafter;
Present mirth hath present laughter.
What's to come is still unsure:
In delay there lies no plenty;
Then come kiss me, sweet and
    twenty,
Youth's a stuff will not endure.

      Shakespeare
      Twelfth-Night, act II, sc. iii, l. 50

Where love is great, the littlest
    doubts are fear;
When little fears grow great, great
    love grows there.

      Shakespeare
      Hamlet, act III, sc. ii, l. 183

      As sweet and musical
As bright Apollo's lute, strung with
    his hair;
And when Love speaks, the voice of
    all the gods
Makes heaven drowsy with the har-
    mony.

      Shakespeare
      Love's Labour's Lost, act IV, sc. iii,
      l. 342

My affection hath an unknown bottom, like the bay of Portugal.

Shakespeare
As You Like It, act IV, sc. i, l. 219

For to be wise, and love,
Exceeds man's might; that dwells
with gods above.

Shakespeare
Troilus and Cressida, act III, sc. ii,
l. 163

In thy face I see
The map of honor, truth, and loyalty.

Shakespeare
King Henry the Sixth, Part II, act III,
sc. i, l. 202

It were all one
That I should love a bright particular
star
And think to wed it, he is so above
me.

Shakespeare
All's Well That Ends Well, act I, sc. i,
l. 97

Let me not to the marriage of true
minds
Admit impediments. Love is not love
Which alters when it alteration finds,
Or bends with the remover to re-
move:
O, no! it is an ever-fixed mark,
That looks on tempest and is never
shaken;
It is the star to every wandering bark,
Whose worth's unknown, although
his height be taken.
Love's not Time's fool, though rosy
lips and cheeks
Within his bending sickle's compass
come;
Love alters not with his brief hours
and weeks,
But bears it out even to the edge of
doom.
If this be error, and upon me prov'd,
I never writ, nor no man ever lov'd.

Shakespeare
Sonnet 116

Music, moody food
Of us that trade in love.

Shakespeare
Antony and Cleopatra, act II, sc. v, l. 1

There are two tragedies in life. One is to lose your heart's desire. The other is to gain it.

George Bernard Shaw
Man and Superman [1903], act IV

Chameleons feed on light and air:
Poets' food is love and fame.

Percy Bysshe Shelley
"An Exhortation" [1819], st. 1

Familiar acts are beautiful through love.

Shelley
Prometheus Unbound [1818–1819],
act IV, l. 403

To suffer woes which Hope thinks
    infinite;
To forgive wrongs darker than death
    or night;
To defy Power, which seems omnip-
    otent;
To love, and bear; to hope till Hope
    creates
From its own wreck the thing it con-
    templates;
Neither to change, nor falter, nor re-
    pent;
This, like thy glory, Titan, is to be
Good, great and joyous, beautiful
    and free;
This is alone Life, Joy, Empire, and
    Victory.

      Shelley
      Ibid. IV, l. 570

The great secret of morals is love; or
    a going out of our own nature,
    and an identification of ourselves
    with the beautiful which exists in
    thought, action, or person not our
    own. . . . The great instrument of
    moral good is the imagination;
    and poetry administers to the
    effect by acting upon the cause.

      Shelley
      A Defense of Poetry [1821]

The one fact that I would cry from every housetop is this: the Good Life is waiting for us — here and now! . . . At this very moment we have the necessary techniques, both material and psychological, to create a full and satisfying life for everyone.

> B. F. Skinner
> *Walden Two* [1948], ch. 23

All's fair in love and war.

> Francis E. Smedley
> *Frank Fairlegh* [1850], ch. 50

There are two things to aim at in life: first, to get what you want; and, after that, to enjoy it. Only the wisest of mankind achieve the second.

> Logan Pearsall Smith
> *Afterthoughts* [1931]

Everything's Coming Up Roses.

> Stephen Sondheim
> *Gypsy* [1959], title of song

One word
Frees us of all the weight and pain of
   life:
That word is love.

> Sophocles
> *Oedipus at Colonus* [406 B.C.], l. 1616

All for love, and nothing for reward.

> Edmund Spenser
> *The Faerie Queen* [1590], bk. II, canto
> 8, st. 2

Fierce wars and faithful loves shall
   moralize my song.

> Spenser
> Ibid. introduction, st. 1

Of all the affections which attend
   human life, the love of glory is the
   most ardent.

> Sir Richard Steele
> *The Spectator*, no 139 [August 9, 1711]

Love has always been the most important business in my life, I should say the only one.

Stendhal
La Vie d'Henri Brulard [1890]

I have lived long enough, having seen one thing, that love hath an end.

Algernon Charles Swinburne
"Hymn to Proserpine" [1866]

The delight that consumes the desire,
The desire that outruns the delight.

Swinburne
"Dolores" [1866], st. 14

To have known love, how bitter a thing it is.

Swinburne
"Laus Veneris" [1866], st. 103

Ah Christ, that it were possible
For one short hour to see
The souls we loved, that they might
   tell us
What and where they be.

> Alfred, Lord Tennyson
> *Maud* [1855], pt. II, sec, iv, st. 3

Ask me no more: thy fate and mine
   are seal'd:
I strove against the stream and all in
   vain:
Let the great river take me to the
   main:
No more, dear love, for at a touch I
   yield;
Ask me no more.

> Tennyson
> *The Princess* [1847], pt. VII. Song, Ask
>   Me No More, st. 3

For a breeze of morning moves,
And the planet of Love is on high,
Beginning to faint in the light that
   she loves
On a bed of daffodil sky.

> Tennyson
> *Maud*, pt. I, sec. xxii, st. 2

Like first love, the heart of Russia
   will not forget you.

   Fëdor Tiutchev
   "Tribute to Pushkin" [January 29,
      1837]

Be good and you will be lonesome.

   Mark Twain
   Following the Equator [1897]. Pudd'n-
      head Wilson's New Calendar, frontis-
      piece caption

Love is and was my lord and king.

   Tennyson
   In Memoriam [1850], 126, st. 1

A man and what he loves and builds
   have but a day and then disap-
   pear; nature cares not — and
   renews the annual round untired.
   It is the old law, sad but not bitter. Only when man destroys the
   life and beauty of nature, there is
   the outrage.

   George M. Trevelyan
   Grey of Fallodon [1937], bk. I, ch. 3

Man is the only animal that
 blushes. Or needs to.

> Mark Twain
> Ibid. ch. 27

Great thoughts come from the
 heart.

> Luc de Clapiers, Marquis de Vauven-
> argues
> *Réflexions et maximes* [c. 1747], no.
> 127

Love that which will never be seen
 twice.

> Alfred de Vigny
> *La Maison du Berger* [1864]

Love conquers all things; let us too
 surrender to Love.

> Virgil
> *Eclogues*, X, l. 69

Change everything, except your loves.

> Voltaire
> *Sur l'Usage de la vie*

Paradise is where I am.

> Voltaire
> *Le Mondain* [1736]

Would you hurt a man keenest, strike at his self-love.

> Lew Wallace
> *Ben Hur: A Tale of the Christ* [1880], bk. VI, ch. 2

My joy, my grief, my hope, my love, Did all within this circle move!

> Edmund Waller
> "On a Girdle" [1664]

The strongest and sweetest songs
   yet remain to be sung.

>Walt Whitman
>*November Boughs* [1888]. A Backward
> Glance O'er Travel'd Roads

It is sweet to dance to violins
When Love and Life are fair:
To dance to flutes, to dance to lutes
Is delicate and rare:
But it is not sweet with nimble feet
To dance upon the air!

>Oscar Wilde
>*The Ballad of Reading Gaol* [1898],
> pt. II, st. 9

   So all we know
Of what they do above
Is that they happy are, and that they
   love.

>Waller
>"Upon the Death of My Lady Rich"
>[1664]

Laugh, and the world laughs with
   you;
Weep, and you weep alone.

>Ella Wheeler Wilcox
>"Solitude," st. 1

Yet each man kills the thing he
    loves,
By each let this be heard,
Some do it with a bitter look,
Some with a flattering word.
The coward does it with a kiss,
The brave man with a sword!

> Wilde
> Ibid. pt. I, st. 7

The only difference between a ca-
    price and a lifelong passion is that
    the caprice lasts a little longer.

> Wilde
> *The Picture of Dorian Gray* [1891],
>   ch. 2

Even memory is not necessary for
    love. There is a land of the living
    and a land of the dead and the
    bridge is love, the only survival,
    the only meaning.

> Thornton Wilder
> *The Bridge of San Luis Rey* [1927], last
>   lines

My advice to you is not to inquire
   why or whither, but just enjoy
   your ice cream while it's on your
   plate — that's my philosophy.

> Wilder
> *The Skin of Our Teeth* [1942], act I

So always look for the silver lining
And try to find the sunny side of life.

> P. G. Wodehouse
> *Sally* [1920]. Look for the Silver Lining

All the things I really like to do are
   either immoral, illegal, or fatten-
   ing.

> Alexander Woollcott
> Remark

   That best portion of a good
      man's life,
His little, nameless, unremembered
   acts
Of kindness and of love.

> William Wordsworth
> "Lines Composed a Few Miles above
>   Tintern Abbey" [1798], l. 33

A pity beyond all telling
Is hid in the heart of love.

> William Butler Yeats
> *The Rose* [1893]. The Pity of Love

Everything that man esteems
Endures a moment or a day.
Love's pleasure drives his love away,
The painter's brush consumes his
    dreams.

> Yeats
> *The Tower* [1928]. Two Songs from a
> Play, II, st. 2

Happy days are here again,
The skies above are clear again:
Let us sing a song of cheer again,
Happy days are here again!

> Jack Yellen
> "Happy Days Are Here Again" [1929]

The love of praise, howe'er con-
    cealed by art,
Reigns more or less, and glows in
    ev'ry heart.

> Edward Young
> *Love of Fame* [1725–1728], satire I,
> l. 51

Marriage

Union gives strength.

> Aesop
> "The Bundle of Sticks"

All the world is queer save me and thee; and sometimes I think thee is a little queer.

> Anonymous
> Attributed to a Quaker, speaking to his wife

Marriage, to women as to men, must be a luxury, not a necessity; an incident of life, not all of it. And the only possible way to accomplish this great change is to accord to women equal power in the making, shaping and controlling of the circumstances of life.

> Susan B. Anthony
> Speech on Social Purity [Spring 1875]

Taking the bull by both horns he kissed her violently on her dainty face. My bride to be he murmured several times.

> Daisy Ashford
> *The Young Visiters* [1919], ch. 9

I married beneath me. All women do.

> Nancy Astor
> Attributed

Wives are young men's mistresses, companions for middle age, and old men's nurses.

> Francis Bacon
> *Essays* [1625]. Of Marriage and Single Life

It is easier to be a lover than a husband for the simple reason that it is more difficult to be witty every day than to say pretty things from time to time.

> Honoré de Balzac
> *Physiologie du mariage* [1829]

Being a husband is a whole-time job.

> Arnold Bennett
> *The Title* [1918], act I

Whoso findeth a wife findeth a good thing.

> The Bible
> Old Testament
> Proverbs 18:22

Who can find a virtuous woman?
  for her price is far above rubies.
The heart of her husband doth
  safely trust in her.

> Old Testament
> Proverbs 31:10–11

Marriage,n. a community consisting
  of a master, a mistress, and two
  slaves, making in all, two.

> Ambrose Bierce
> *The Devil's Dictionary* [1906]

Life does not give itself to one who
  tries to keep all its advantages at
  once. I have often thought moral-
  ity may perhaps consist solely in
  the courage of making a choice.

> Léon Blum
> "On Marriage"

To have and to hold from this day
  forward, for better for worse, for
  richer for poorer, in sickness and
  in health, to love and to cherish,
  till death us do part.

> The Book of Common Prayer [1928]
> Solemnization of Matrimony

With this Ring I thee wed.

> The Book of Common Prayer
> Ibid.

Those whom God hath joined together let no man put asunder.

> The Book of Common Prayer
> Ibid.

If ever two were one, then surely
we.
If ever man were loved by wife, then
thee;
If ever wife was happy in a man,
Compare with me ye women if you
can.

> Anne Bradstreet
> "To My Dear and Loving Husband"
> [1678]

He [Brigham Young] is dreadfully
married. He's the most married
man I ever saw in my life.

> Charles Farrar Browne [Artemus
> Ward]
> *Artemus Ward's Lecture* [1866]

Grow old along with me!
The best is yet to be,
The last of life, for which the first was
    made.
Our times are in his hand.

> Robert Browning
> *Rabbi Ben Ezra* [1864], st. 1

It was very good of God to let Carlyle and Mrs. Carlyle marry one
another and so make only two
people miserable instead of four.

> Samuel Butler
> Letter to Miss E. M. A. Savage
> [November 21, 1884]

Love and marriage, love and mar-
    riage,
Go together like a horse and carriage.

> Sammy Cahn
> *Our Town* (television musical) [1955].
> Love and Marriage

My heart is wax molded as she
pleases, but enduring as marble
to retain.

> Miguel de Cervantes
> *The Little Gypsy (La Gitanilla)*

Those two fatal words, Mine and
  Thine.

> Cervantes
> *Don Quixote de la Mancha*, pt. I
> [1605], bk. II, ch. 3

Promise is most given when the
  least is said.

> George Chapman
> *Hero and Leander* [1598]

The day after that wedding night I
  found that a distance of a thousand miles, abyss and discovery
  and irremediable metamorphosis,
  separated me from the day before.

> Colette
> *Noces* [1945]

Daisy, Daisy, give me your answer,
  do!
I'm half crazy, all for the love of you!
It won't be a stylish marriage,
I can't afford a carriage,
But you'll look sweet upon the seat
Of a bicycle built for two!

> Harry Dacre
> "Daisy Bell" [1892]

Here must all distrust be left behind; all cowardice must be
  ended.

> Dante Alighieri
> *The Divine Comedy* [c. 1310–1321].
> Inferno, canto III, l. 14

'Twas my one Glory —
Let it be
Remembered
I was owned of Thee —

> Emily Dickinson
> No. 1028 [c. 1865]

Man and woman are two locked
  caskets, of which each contains
  the key to the other.

> Isak Dinesen
> *Winter Tales* [1942]. A Consolatory
> Tale

That old saying which the peasants
  call the bachelors' prayer: "I pray
  thee, good Lord, that I may not
  be married. But if I am to be married, that I may not be a cuckold.
  But if I am to be a cuckold, that I
  may not know. But if I am to
  know, that I may not mind."

> Dinesen
> *Seven Gothic Tales* [1934]. The Poet

And dare love that, and say so too,
And forget the He and She.

> John Donne
> "The Undertaking," st. 5

Come live with me, and be my love,
And we will some new pleasures
  prove
Of golden sands, and crystal brooks,
With silken lines, and silver hooks.

> Donne
> "The Bait," st.1

I wonder by my troth, what thou,
    and I
Did, till we lov'd? were we not wean'd
    till then?
But suck'd on country pleasures,
    childishly?
Or snorted we in the seven sleepers'
    den?

> Donne
> "The Good Morrow," st. 1

If they be two, they are two so
As stiff twin compasses are two,
Thy soul the fixt foot, makes no show
To move, but doth, if the other do.

> Donne
> "A Valediction Forbidding Mourning,"
>   st. 7

Our eye-beams twisted, and did
    thread
Our eyes, upon one double string;
So to entergraft our hands, as yet
Was all the means to make us one,
And pictures in our eyes to get
Was all our propagation.

> Donne
> "The Extasy," l. 7

Our two souls therefore which are
    one,
Though I must go, endure not yet
A breach, but an expansion,
Like gold to airy thinness beat.

> Donne
> "A Valediction Forbidding Mourning,"
> st. 6

Man's best possession is a sympa-
thetic wife.

> Euripides
> *Antigone*, fragment 164

Let's Call the Whole Thing Off!

> Ira Gershwin
> *Shall We Dance* [1937], title of song

Let there be spaces in your togeth-
erness.

> Kahlil Gibran
> *The Prophet* [1923]. On Marriage

For I'm not so old, and not so plain,
And I'm quite prepared to marry
    again.

> Sir William S. Gilbert
> *Iolanthe* [1882], act I

None shall part us from each other,
One in life and death are we:
All in all to one another —
I to thee and thou to me!
Thou the tree and I the flower —
Thou the idol; I the throng —
Thou the day and I the hour —
Thou the singer; I the song!

Gilbert
Ibid.

Prithee, pretty maiden, will you
   marry me?
(Hey, but I'm hopeful, willow, willow, waly!)

Gilbert
Patience [1881], act I

The sum which two married people
   owe to one another defies calcu-
   lation. It is an infinite debt,
   which can only be discharged
   through all eternity.

Johann Wolfgang von Goethe
Elective Affinities [1808], bk. I, ch. 9

I . . . chose my wife, as she did her wedding gown, not for a fine glossy surface, but such qualities as would wear well.

> Oliver Goldsmith
> *The Vicar of Wakefield* [1766], ch. 1

Two souls with but a single thought,
Two hearts that beat as one.

> Friedrich Halm
> *Der Sohn der Wildness* [1842], act II

Collaborating in the very private way of love or the highest kind of friendship . . . is the way for gifted, energetic wives of writers to a sort of composition of their own, this peculiar illusion of collaboration.

> Elizabeth Hardwick
> *Seduction and Betrayal: Women in Literature* [1974]. Amateurs

The fundamental error of their matrimonial union; that of having based a permanent contract on a temporary feeling.

> Thomas Hardy
> *Jude the Obscure* [1895], pt. I, ch. 11

You and me, we've made a separate peace.

> Ernest Hemingway
> *In Our Time* [1924], ch. 6

Couples are wholes and not wholes, what agrees disagrees, the concordant is discordant. From all things one and from one all things.

> Heraclitus
> *On the Universe*, fragment 59

The critical period in matrimony is breakfast-time.

> Sir Alan Patrick Herbert
> *Uncommon Law* [1935], p. 98

I sing of brooks, of blossoms, birds, and bowers:
Of April, May, of June, and July flowers.
I sing of Maypoles, Hock-carts, wassails, wakes,
Of bridegrooms, brides, and of their bridal cakes.

> Robert Herrick
> *Hesperides* [1648]. Argument of His Book

Washington is full of famous men
  and the women they married
  when they were young.

> Fanny Dixwell Holmes
> From Catherine Drinker Bowen,
>   *Yankee from Olympus* [1944]

God always pairs off like with like.

> Homer
> *The Odyssey*, bk. XVII, l. 218

Therefore don't you be gentle to
  your wife either. Don't tell her
  everything you know, but tell her
  one thing and keep another thing
  hidden.

> Homer
> Ibid. bk. XI, l. 441

May the gods grant you all things
which your heart desires, and
may they give you a husband and
a home and gracious concord, for
there is nothing greater and better than this — when a husband
and wife keep a household in
oneness of mind, a great woe to
their enemies and joy to their
friends, and win high renown.

> Homer
> Ibid. bk. VI, l. 180

To have — to hold — and — in
time — let go!

> Laurence Hope
> *India's Love Lyrics*. The Teak Forest,
> st. 10

Happy, thrice happy and more, are
they whom an unbroken bond
unites and whose love shall know
no sundering quarrels so long as
they shall live.

> Horace
> *Odes*, bk. I, xiii, l. 17

With you I should love to live, with
  you be ready to die.

> Horace
> Ibid. bk. III, ix, last line

Happy bridegroom, Hesper brings
All desired and timely things.
All whom morning sends to roam,
Hesper loves to lead them home.
Home return who him behold,
Child to mother, sheep to fold,
Bird to nest from wandering wide:
Happy bridegroom, seek your bride.

> A. E. Housman
> *Last Poems* [1922], 24 (Epithalamium),
> st. 3

Drink to me only with thine eyes,
And I will pledge with mine;
Or leave a kiss but in the cup
And I'll not look for wine.
The thirst that from the soul doth rise
Doth ask a drink divine;
But might I of Jove's nectar sup,
I would not change for thine.

> Ben Jonson
> *The Forest* [1616]. To Celia, st. 1

In every house of marriage
there's room for an interpreter.

> Stanley Kunitz
> "Route Six" [1979]

This is John Thomas marryin' Lady
Jane.

> D. H. Lawrence
> *Lady Chatterley's Lover* [1928]

Get me to the church on time!

> Alan Jay Lerner
> *My Fair Lady* [1956], act II, Get Me to
> the Church on Time

I could not love thee, dear, so
  much,
Lov'd I not honor more.

> Richard Lovelace
> *Lucasta* [1649]. To Lucasta: Going to
> the Wars, st. 3

There is no more lovely, friendly
and charming relationship, communion or company than a good
marriage.

> Martin Luther
> *Table Talk* [1569], 292

Marriages are made in heaven and consummated on earth.

> John Lyly
> *Mother Bombie* [1590], act IV, sc. i

Come live with me, and be my love;
And we will all the pleasures prove
That valleys, groves, hills, and fields,
Woods or steepy mountain yields.

> Christopher Marlowe
> "The Passionate Shepherd to His Love"
> [c. 1589]

Love is . . . born with the pleasure of looking at each other, it is fed with the necessity of seeing each other, it is concluded with the impossibility of separation!

> José Martí
> *Amor* [1881]

You're obstinate, pliant, merry, morose, all at once. For me there's no living with you, or without you.

> Martial
> *Epigrams*, XII, 47

Marriage, if one will face the truth,
   is an evil, but a necessary evil.

> Menander
> Unidentified fragment 651

Hail wedded love, mysterious law,
   true source
Of human offspring.

> John Milton
> *Paradise Lost*, bk. IV, l. 750

Our state cannot be sever'd; we are
   one,
One flesh; to lose thee were to lose
   myself.

> Milton
> Ibid. bk. IX, l. 958

Live while ye may,
Yet happy pair.

> Milton
> Ibid. bk. IV, l. 533

I wonder what Adam and Eve
think of it by this time.

> Marianne Moore
> "Marriage" [1935]

Let woman then go on — not asking favors, but claiming as a right the removal of all hindrances to her elevation in the scale of being — let her receive encouragement for the proper cultivation of all her powers, so that she may enter profitably into the active business of life. . . .Then in the marriage union, the independence of the husband and wife will be equal, their dependence mutual, and their obligations reciprocal.

> Lucretia Mott
> "Discourse on Woman" [delivered December 17, 1849], last paragraph

He tells you when you've got on too much lipstick,
And helps you with your girdle when your hips stick.

> Ogden Nash
> *Versus* [1949]. The Perfect Husband

I believe a little incompatibility is the spice of life, particularly if he has income and she is pattable.

> Nash
> Ibid. I Do, I Will, I Have

Give me, next good, an understanding wife,
By nature wise, not learned much by
art.

> Sir Thomas Overbury
> *A Wife* [1614]

So I can't live either without you or
with you.

> Ovid
> *Amores*, III, xi, 39

A Woman is a foreign land,
Of which, though there he settle
young,
A man will ne'er quite understand
The customs, politics, and tongue.

> Coventry Patmore
> *The Angel in the House* [1854–1856],
> bk. I, canto 9. Prelude 2, Woman

What is yours is mine, and all mine
is yours.

> Plautus
> *Trinummus*, act II, sc. ii, l. 48

Advice to persons about to
marry. — "Don't."

> *Punch*, vol. VIII, p. 1 [1845]

Always contented with his life,
and with his dinner, and his wife.

> Alexander Pushkin
> *Eugene Onegin* [1823], ch. 1, st.12

Let all thy joys be as the month of
　May,
And all thy days be as a marriage day:
Let sorrow, sickness, and a troubled
　mind
Be stranger to thee.

> Francis Quarles
> "To a Bride"

If all the world and love were
　young,
And truth in every shepherd's
　tongue,
These pretty pleasures might me
　move
To live with thee, and be thy love.

> Sir Walter Ralegh
> "The Nymph's Reply to the Passionate
> Shepherd" (printed in *England's Heli-
> con*) [1600], st. 1

A good marriage is that in which each appoints the other guardian of his solitude.

> Rainer Maria Rilke
> *Letters*

Life in common among people who love each other is the ideal of happiness.

> George Sand
> *Histoire de ma vie* [1856]

You roll my log, and I will roll yours.

> Seneca
> *Apocolocyntosis*, sec. 9

Kiss me, Kate, we will be married o' Sunday.

> William Shakespeare
> *The Taming of the Shrew*, act II, sc. i,
> l. 318

Now join your hands, and with your hands your hearts.

> Shakespeare
> *King Henry the Sixth, Part III*, act IV,
> sc. vi, l. 39

You are my true and honorable wife,
As dear to me as are the ruddy drops
That visit my sad heart.

> Shakespeare
> *Julius Caesar*, act II, sc. i, l. 288

Wives may be merry, and yet honest
too.

> Shakespeare
> *The Merry Wives of Windsor*, act IV,
> sc. ii, l. 110

What's mine is yours, and what is
yours is mine.

> Shakespeare
> *Measure for Measure* [1604], act V,
> sc. i, l. 539

Men are April when they woo, December when they wed: maids
are May when they are maids, but
the sky changes when they are
wives.

> Shakespeare
> *As You Like It*, act IV, sc. i, l. 153

So we grew together,
Like to a double cherry, seeming parted,
But yet an union in partition;
Two lovely berries molded on one stem.

Shakespeare
A Midsummer-Night's Dream, act III,
sc. ii, l. 208

Marriage is popular because it combines the maximum of temptation with the maximum of opportunity.

George Bernard Shaw
Man and Superman [1903]. Maxims for Revolutionists

When two people are under the influence of the most violent, most insane, most delusive, and most transient of passions, they are required to swear that they will remain in that excited, abnormal, and exhausting condition continuously until death do them part.

Shaw
Getting Married [1908], preface

'Tis safest in matrimony to begin
   with a little aversion.

>   Richard Brinsley Sheridan
>   *The Rivals* [1775], act I, sc. ii

You had no taste when you married
   me.

>   Sheridan
>   *The School for Scandal* [1777], act I,
>   sc. ii

My dear, my better half.

>   Sir Philip Sidney
>   *The Arcadia* [written 1580], bk. III

A little in drink, but at all times yr
   faithful husband.

>   Sir Richard Steele
>   *Letters to His Wife* [September 27,
>   1708]

The union of hands and hearts.

>   Jeremy Taylor
>   *Sermons* [1653]. The Marriage Ring,
>   pt. I

If there were no internal propensity
to unite, even at a prodigiously
rudimentary level — indeed in
the molecule itself — it would be
physically impossible for love to
appear higher up.

Pierre Teilhard de Chardin
The Phenomenon of Man [1959], bk.
IV, ch. 2, sec. 2

Harmony is pure love, for love is
complete agreement.

Lope de Vega
Fuenteovejuna [1613], act I, l. 381

Who was that lady I saw you with
last night?
She ain't no lady; she's my wife.

Joseph Weber and Lew Fields
Vaudeville routine [1887]

In the choice of a horse and a wife,
a man must please himself, ignor-
ing the opinion and advice of
friends.

George John Whyte-Melville
"Riding Recollections" [1878]

Most everybody in the world climbs
　into their graves married.

> Thornton Wilder
> *Our Town* [1938], act II

The best part of married life is the
　fights. The rest is merely so-so.

> Wilder
> *The Matchmaker* [1954], act II

He first deceased; she for a little
　tried
To live without him, liked it not, and
　died.

> Sir Henry Wotton
> "Upon the Death of Sir Albert Morton's
> Wife" [1651]

Take my wife . . . please!

> Henny Youngman
> Comedy line

Family and Friendship

Accident counts for much in companionship as in marriage.

> Henry Adams
> *The Education of Henry Adams* [1907],
> ch. 4

Friends are born, not made.

> Adams
> Ibid. ch. 7

One friend in a lifetime is much; two are many; three are hardly possible. Friendship needs a certain parallelism of life, a community of thought, a rivalry of aim.

> Adams
> Ibid. ch. 20

What is a friend? A single soul dwelling in two bodies.

> Aristotle
> From Diogenes Laertius, *Lives of Eminent Philosophers*, bk. V, sec. 20

Is it so small a thing
To have enjoyed the sun,
To have lived light in the spring,
To have loved, to have thought, to
    have done;
To have advanced true friends, and
    beat down baffling foes?

> Matthew Arnold
> *Empedocles on Etna* [1852], act II,
> sc. ii, l. 397

To live happily with other people
    one should ask of them only what
    they can give.

> Tristan Bernard
> *L'Enfant prodigue du Vesinet* [1921]

Shall we make a new rule of life
    from tonight: always to try to be a
    little kinder than is necessary?

> Sir James M. Barrie
> *The Little White Bird* [1902], ch. 4

A man that hath friends must show
    himself friendly: and there is a
    friend that sticketh closer than a
    brother.

> The Bible
> Old Testament
> Proverbs 18:24

And Jonathan . . . loved him
  [David] as he loved his own soul.

> Old Testament
> I Samuel 20:17

As one whom his mother comforteth, so will I comfort you.

> Old Testament
> Isaiah 66:13

I love them that love me; and those
  that seek me early shall find me.

> Old Testament
> Proverbs 8:17

In her tongue is the law of kindness.
She looketh well to the ways of her
  household, and eateth not the
  bread of idleness.
Her children arise up, and call her
  blessed.

> Old Testament
> Proverbs 31:26–28

Thou shalt love thy neighbor as thyself.

> Old Testament
> Leviticus 19:18

Thy love to me was wonderful,
   passing the love of women.
How are the mighty fallen, and the
   weapons of war perished!

> Old Testament
> II Samuel 1:26–27

A faithful friend is a strong defense:
   and he that hath found such an
   one hath found a treasure.

> Apocrypha
> The Wisdom of Jesus the Son of
>   Sirach, or Ecclesiasticus 6:14

A faithful friend is the medicine of
   life.

> Apocrypha
> The Wisdom of Jesus the Son of
>   Sirach, or Ecclesiasticus 6:16

A new commandment I give unto
   you, That ye love one another.

> New Testament
> John 13:34

Be kindly affectioned one to another with brotherly love.

> New Testament
> Romans 12:10

Owe no man anything, but to love
  one another.

> New Testament
> Romans 13: 7–8

Beareth all things, believeth all
  things, hopeth all things, en-
  dureth all things.
Charity never faileth.

> New Testament
> I Corinthians 13: 7–8

For I was an hungred, and ye gave
  me meat: I was thirsty, and ye
  gave me drink: I was a stranger,
  and ye took me in:
Naked, and ye clothed me: I was
  sick, and ye visited me: I was in
  prison, and ye came unto me.

> New Testament
> Matthew 25:35–36

God loveth a cheerful giver.

> New Testament
> II Corinthians 9:7

Let brotherly love continue.
Be not forgetful to entertain strangers: for thereby some have entertained angels unawares.

> New Testament
> Hebrews 13:1–2

We that had loved him so, followed him, honored him,
Lived in his mild and magnificent eye,
Learned his great language, caught his clear accents,
Made him our pattern to live and to die!

> Robert Browning
> "The Lost Leader" [1845], st. 1

Let love be without dissimulation.

> New Testament
> Romans 12:9

"Friendship is Love without his wings!"

> Lord Byron
> "L'Amitie Est l'Amour sans Ailes"
> [written 1806]

What's the Constitution between
   friends?

> Timothy J. Campbell
> Attributed [c. 1885]

How to Win Friends and Influence
   People.

> Dale Carnegie
> Title of book [1938]

Child of the pure, unclouded brow
And dreaming eyes of wonder!
Though time be fleet and I and thou
Are half a life asunder,
Thy loving smile will surely hail
The love-gift of a fairy tale.

> Lewis Carroll
> *Through the Looking-Glass* [1872],
>   introduction, st. 1

One sweetly solemn thought
Comes to me o'er and o'er;
I am nearer home today
Than I ever have been before.

> Phoebe Cary
> "Nearer Home," st. 1

Only solitary men know the full joys
of friendship. Others have their
family; but to a solitary and an
exile his friends are everything.

> Willa Cather
> *Shadows on the Rock* [1931], bk. III,
> ch. 5

My love and hers have always been
purely Platonic.

> Miguel de Cervantes
> *Don Quixote de la Mancha*, pt. I
> [1605], bk. III, ch. 11

To an open house in the evening
Home shall men come,
To an older place than Eden
And a taller town than Rome.

> G. K. Chesterton
> "The House of Christmas"

Every murderer is probably somebody's old friend.

> Agatha Christie
> *The Mysterious Affair at Styles* [1920],
> ch. 11

A friend is, as it were, a second self.

> Cicero
> *De Amicitia*, XXI

Flowers are lovely; love is flower-
   like;
Friendship is a sheltering tree.

> Samuel Taylor Coleridge
> "Youth and Age" [1823–1832], st. 2

The happiness of life is made up of
   minute fractions — the little soon
   forgotten charities of a kiss or
   smile, a kind look, a heartfelt
   compliment, and the countless
   infinitesimals of pleasurable and
   genial feeling.

> Coleridge
> *The Friend*. The Improvisatore [1828]

Ever been the best of friends!

> Charles Dickens
> *Great Expectations* [1860–1861],
>   ch. 18

Elysium is as far as to
The very nearest Room
If in that Room a Friend await
Felicity or Doom —

What Fortitude the Soul contains,
That it can so endure
The accent of a coming Foot —
The opening of a Door —

> Emily Dickinson
> No. 1760 [n.d.]

If I can stop one Heart from break-
  ing
I shall not live in vain
If I can ease one Life the Aching
Or cool one Pain
Or help one fainting Robin
Unto his Nest again
I shall not live in Vain.

> Dickinson
> No. 919 [c. 1864]

Some keep the Sabbath going to
   Church —
I keep it, staying at Home —
With a bobolink for a Chorister —
And an Orchard, for a Dome —

> Dickinson
> No. 324 [1862], st. 1

A little work, a little play,
To keep us going — and so, good
   day!
A little warmth, a little light,
Of love's bestowing — and so, good
   night!
A little fun, to match the sorrow
Of each day's growing — and so,
   good morrow!
A little trust that when we die
We reap our sowing! and so — good-
   bye!

> George du Maurier
> *Trilby* [1894], pt. VIII

A friend is a person with whom I
   may be sincere. Before him, I
   may think aloud.

> Ralph Waldo Emerson
> *Essays: First Series* [1841]. Friendship

A friend may well be reckoned the
    masterpiece of Nature.

        Emerson
        Ibid.

Happy is the house that shelters a
    friend.

        Emerson
        Ibid.

I do then with my friends as I do
    with my books. I would have
    them where I can find them, but
    I seldom use them.

        Emerson
        Ibid.

The only reward of virtue is virtue;
    the only way to have a friend is to
    be one.

        Emerson
        Ibid.

It is in the thirties that we want
    friends. In the forties we know
    they won't save us any more than
    love did.

        F. Scott Fitzgerald
        Notebooks [1978]

Of all the icy blasts that blow on
love, a request for money is the
most chilling and havoc-
wreaking.

> Gustave Flaubert
> *Madame Bovary* [1857], pt. III, ch. 8

If I had to choose between betraying my country and betraying my
friend, I hope I should have the
guts to betray my country.

> E. M. Forster
> *Two Cheers for Democracy* [1951].
> What I Believe

Only connect! That was the whole
of her sermon. Only connect the
prose and the passion, and both
will be exalted, and human love
will be seen at its height. Live in
fragments no longer. Only connect, and the beast and the
monk, robbed of the isolation that
is life to either, will die.

> Forster
> *Howards End* [1910], ch. 22

Let me live in my house by the side
of the road
And be a friend to man.

> Sam Walter Foss
> "The House by the Side of the Road,"
> st. 5

If a man has been his mother's un-
disputed darling he retains
throughout life the triumphant
feeling, the confidence in success, which not seldom brings
actual success with it.

> Sigmund Freud
> *A Childhood Memory of Goethe's* [1917]

Home is the place where, when you
have to go there,
They have to take you in.

> Robert Frost
> *The Death of the Hired Man* [1914]

No memory of having starred
Atones for later disregard,
Or keeps the end from being hard.

Better to go down dignified
With boughten friendship by your
  side
Than none at all. Provide, provide!

> Frost
> "Provide, Provide" [1936], st. 6, 7

The greatest thing in family life is to
  take a hint when a hint is intended — and not to take a hint
  when a hint isn't intended.

> Frost
> Comment

I love my fellow creatures — I do
  all the good I can —
Yet everybody says I'm such a dis-
  agreeable man!
And I can't think why!

> Sir William S. Gilbert
> *Princess Ida* [1884], act I

Friendship is a disinterested commerce between equals; love, an abject intercourse between tyrants and slaves.

> Oliver Goldsmith
> *The Good-Natur'd Man* [1768], act I

Green be the turf above thee,
Friend of my better days!
None knew thee but to love thee,
Nor named thee but to praise.

> Fitz-Greene Halleck
> "On the Death of Joseph Rodman
> Drake" [1820], st. 1

Even in the common affairs of life, in love, friendship, and marriage, how little security have we when we trust our happiness in the hands of others!

> William Hazlitt
> *Table Talk* [1821–1822]. On Living to
> One's Self

Why should good words ne'er be
    said
Of a friend till he is dead?

> Daniel Webster Hoyt
> "A Sermon in Rhyme" [1878], st. 1

Justice is the only worship.
Love is the only priest.
Ignorance is the only slavery.
Happiness is the only good.
The time to be happy is now,
The place to be happy is here,
The way to be happy is to make
    others so.

> Robert Green Ingersoll
> Creed

Well, we all need someone we can
    lean on,
And if you want it, well, you can lean
    on me.

> Mick Jagger and Keith Richards
> "Let it Bleed" [1969]

Let your boat of life be light,
packed with only what you
need — a homely home and simple pleasures, one or two friends,
worth the name, someone to love
and someone to love you, a cat, a
dog, and a pipe or two, enough to
eat and enough to wear, and a
little more than enough to drink;
for thirst is a dangerous thing.

Jerome K. Jerome
Three Men in a Boat [1889], ch. 3

The endearing elegance of female
friendship.

Samuel Johnson
Rasselas [1759], ch. 46

I loved the man [Shakespeare] and
do honor his memory, on this side
idolatry, as much as any.

Ben Jonson
*Timber; or, Discoveries Made upon Men
and Matter* [1640]

True happiness
Consists not in the multitude of
  friends,
But in the worth and choice.

> Jonson
> *Cynthia's Revels* [1600], act III, sc. ii

The crown of these
Is made of love and friendship, and
  sits high
Upon the forehead of humanity.

> John Keats
> *Endymion* [1818], bk. I, l. 800

Little Friend of All the World.

> Rudyard Kipling
> *Kim* [1901], ch. 1

We're tenting tonight on the old
  campground,
Give us a song to cheer
Our weary hearts, a song of home
And friends we love so dear.

> Walter Kittredge
> "Tenting on the Old Campground"
>   [1864], st. 1

Sociability is as much a law of nature as mutual struggle . . . mutual aid is as much a law of animal life as mutual struggle.

> Prince Pëtr Kropotkin
> *Mutual Aid* [1902]

We always like those who admire us; we do not always like those whom we admire.

> François, Duc de la Rochefoucauld
> *Reflections; or, Sentences and Moral Maxims* [1678], maxim 294

We pardon to the extent that we love.

> La Rochefoucauld
> Ibid. 330

You love me so much, you want to put me in your pocket. And I should die there smothered.

> D. H. Lawrence
> *Sons and Lovers* [1913], ch. 15

And the song, from beginning to end,
I found again in the heart of a friend.

> Henry Wadsworth Longfellow
> "The Arrow and the Song" [1845], st. 3

I want, by understanding myself, to understand others. I want to be all that I am capable of becoming. . . . This all sounds very strenuous and serious. But now that I have wrestled with it, it's no longer so. I feel happy — deep down. *All is well.*

> Katherine Mansfield
> *Journal* [1922], last entry

It is man's peculiar duty to love even those who wrong him.

> Marcus Aurelius
> *Meditations*, VII, 22

Very little is needed to make a happy life.

> Marcus Aurelius
> Ibid. 67

Degenerate sons and daughters,
Life is too strong for you —
It takes life to love life.

> Edgar Lee Masters
> *Spoon River Anthology* [1915]. Lucinda Matlock

People, people who need people
Are the luckiest people in the world.

> Bob Merrill
> "People" [1963]

It is a wonderful seasoning of all
    enjoyments to think of those we
    love.

> Molière
> *Le Misanthrope* [1666], act V, sc. iv

My fair one, let us swear an eternal
    friendship.

> Molière
> *Le Bourgeois Gentilhomme* [1670], act
>   IV, sc. i

The more we love our friends, the
    less we flatter them; it is by ex-
    cusing nothing that pure love
    shows itself.

> Molière
> *Le Misanthrope*, act II, sc. v

Oh, call it by some better name,
For friendship sounds too cold.

> Thomas Moore
> *Ballads and Songs*. Oh, Call It by Some
>   Better Name, st. 1

The moonlight is the softest, in
    Kentucky,
Summer days come oftest, in Ken-
    tucky,
    Friendship is the strongest,
    Love's fires glow the longest,
    Yet a wrong is always wrongest,
In Kentucky.

> James H. Mulligan
> "In Kentucky," st. 1

Each friend represents a world in
    us, a world possibly not born until
    they arrive, and it is only by this
    meeting that a new world is born.

> Anaïs Nin
> *The Diary of Anaïs Nin*, vol. II [1967],
>   March 1937

This is the hardest of all: to close
    the open hand out of love, and
    keep modest as a giver.

> Friedrich Nietzsche
> *Thus Spake Zarathustra* [1883–1891],
>   pt. II, ch. 23

So long as you are secure you will
count many friends; if your life
becomes clouded you will be
alone.

> Ovid
> *Tristia*, I, ix, 5

To know when one's self is inter-
ested, is the first condition of
interesting other people.

> Walter Pater
> *Marius the Epicurean* [1885], ch. 6

He who loves me, let him follow
me.

> Philip VI
> Attributed

Friends have all things in common.

> Plato
> *Dialogues*. Phaedrus, sec. 279

Nothing is there more friendly to a
man than a friend in need.

> Plautus
> *Epidicus*, act III, sc. iii, l. 44

Thou wert my guide, philosopher, and friend.

> Alexander Pope
> *An Essay on Man* [1733–1734]. Epistle IV, l. 390

My Heart Belongs to Daddy.

> Cole Porter
> *Leave It to Me* [1938], title of song

The bonds that unite another person to ourself exist only in our mind. Memory as it grows fainter relaxes them, and notwithstanding the illusion by which we would fain be cheated and with which, out of love, friendship, politeness, deference, duty, we cheat other people, we exist alone. Man is the creature that cannot emerge from himself, that knows his fellows only in himself; when he asserts the contrary, he is lying.

> Marcel Proust
> *Remembrance of Things Past* [1913–1927]. *The Sweet Cheat Gone*

What thou lovest well remains, the
  rest is dross
What thou lov'st well shall not be reft
  from thee
What thou lov'st well is thy true her-
  itage
Whose world, or mine or theirs or is it
  of none?
First came the seen, then thus the
  palpable
        Elysium, though it were in
  the halls of hell.
What thou lovest well is thy true her-
  itage.

> Ezra Pound
> *Cantos* [1925–1959], LXXXI

Never change when love has found
  its home.

> Sextus Propertius
> *Elegies,* I, i, 36

Give a little love to a child, and you
  get a great deal back.

> John Ruskin
> *The Crown of Wild Olive* [1866],
>   lecture 1

The sacrifices of friendship were
   beautiful in her eyes as long as
   she was not asked to make them.

> Saki
> *Beasts and Super-Beasts* [1914]. Fur

To like and dislike the same things,
   that is indeed true friendship.

> Sallust
> *The War with Catiline* [c. 40 B.C.],
>   sec. 20

True friendship is never serene.

> Marie de Rabutin-Chantal, Marquise
>   de Sévigné
> *Lettres.* À Madame de Grignan,
>   [September 10, 1671]

Friendship is constant in all other
   things
Save in the office and affairs of love:
Therefore all hearts in love use their
   own tongues;
Let every eye negotiate for itself
And trust no agent.

> William Shakespeare
> *Much Ado About Nothing*, act II, sc. i,
> l. 184

I count myself in nothing else so
   happy
As in a soul remembering my good
   friends.

> Shakespeare
> *King Richard the Second*, act II, sc. iii,
> l. 46

In following him, I follow but myself.

> Shakespeare
> *Othello*, act I, sc. i, l. 58

That is my home of love: if I have
   rang'd,
Like him that travels, I return again.

> Shakespeare
> Sonnet 109, l. 5

To me, fair friend, you never can be
  old,
For as you were when first your eye I
  ey'd,
Such seems your beauty still.

Shakespeare
Sonnet 104, l. 1

I do not ask you much:
I beg cold comfort.

Shakespeare
King John, act V, sc. vii, l. 41

Love all, trust a few,
Do wrong to none: be able for thine
  enemy
Rather in power than use, and keep
  thy friend
Under thy own life's key: be check'd
  for silence,
But never tax'd for speech.

Shakespeare
All's Well That Ends Well, act I, sc. i,
l. 74

Unkindness may do much;
And his unkindness may defeat my
   life,
But never taint my love.

   Shakespeare
   Othello, act IV, sc. ii, l. 159

We have no more right to consume
   happiness without producing it
   than to consume wealth without
   producing it.

   George Bernard Shaw
   Candida [1898], act I

So long as we love we serve; so long
   as we are loved by others, I would
   almost say that we are indispens-
   able; and no man is useless while
   he has a friend.

   Robert Louis Stevenson
   Across the Plains [1892]. Lay Morals

The sight of you is good for sore
   eyes.

   Jonathan Swift
   Polite Conversation [1738], dialogue 1

What is the price of a thousand
  horses against a son where there
  is one son only?

> John Millington Synge
> *Riders to the Sea* [1904]

Charity begins at home.

> Terence
> *Andria (The Lady of Andros)*, l. 635

See how these Christians love one
  another.

> Tertullian
> *Apologeticus*, 39

Verily great grace may go
With a little gift; and precious are all
  things that come from friends.

> Theocritus
> *Idylls*, XXVIII

Happy families are all alike; every
unhappy family is unhappy in its
own way.

> Leo Tolstoi
> *Anna Karenina* [1875–1877], pt. I,
> ch. 1

The holy passion of Friendship is of
so sweet and steady and loyal and
enduring a nature that it will last
through a whole lifetime, if not
asked to lend money.

> Mark Twain
> *Pudd'nhead Wilson* [1894]. Pudd'nhead
> Wilson's Calendar, ch. 8

The young need old men. They
need men who are not ashamed
of age, not pathetic imitations of
themselves. . . . Parents are the
bones on which children sharpen
their teeth.

> Peter Ustinov
> *Dear Me* [1977], ch. 18

The one absolutely unselfish friend that man can have in this selfish world, the one that never deserts him, the one that never proves ungrateful or treacherous, is his dog. . . . When all other friends desert, he remains.

George Graham Vest
Speech in the Senate [1884]

I die adoring God, loving my friends, not hating my enemies, and detesting superstition.

Voltaire
Written February 28, 1778

Whatever you do, crush the infamous thing [superstition], and love those who love you.

Voltaire
Letter to d'Alembert [November 28, 1762]

The hand that rocks the cradle
Is the hand that rules the world.

> William Ross Wallace
> "The Hand That Rules the World,"
> st. 1

I love such mirth as does not make
　friends ashamed to look upon one
　another next morning.

> Izaak Walton
> *The Compleat Angler* [1653–1655],
> pt. I, ch. 5

None of the new spiders ever quite
　took her place in his heart. She
　was in a class by herself. It is not
　often that someone comes along
　who is a true friend and a good
　writer. Charlotte was both.

> E. B. White
> *Charlotte's Web* [1952], ch. 22

Children begin by loving their par-
　ents; as they grow older they
　judge them; sometimes they for-
　give them.

> Oscar Wilde
> *The Picture of Dorian Gray* [1891],
> ch. 5

If all the good people were clever,
And all clever people were good,
The world would be nicer than ever
We thought that it possibly could.

> Elizabeth Wordsworth
> "Good and Clever" [1890]

Father, dear father, come home
   with me now,
The clock in the belfry strikes one;
You said you were coming right home
   from the shop
As soon as your day's work was done.

> Henry Clay Work
> "Come Home, Father" [1864], st. 1

[When asked, "What is a friend?"]
   Another I.

> Zeno
> From Diogenes Laertius, *Lives of Eminent Philosophers*, bk. VII, sec. 23

God, Country,
the World

All things bright and beautiful,
All creatures great and small,
All things wise and wonderful,
The Lord God made them all.

> Cecil Frances Alexander
> "All Things Bright and Beautiful"
> [1848], st. 1

O our Mother the Earth, O our
  Father the Sky,
Your children are we, and with tired
  backs
We bring you gifts.

> Anonymous North American Indian;
> Song of the Sky Loom (Tewa)

How many are your deeds,
Though hidden from sight,
O Sole God beside whom there is
  none!
You made the earth as you wished,
  you alone.

> The Great Hymn to the Aten, st. 5

The King of love my shepherd is,
Whose goodness faileth never;
I nothing lack if I am his,
And he is mine, forever.

> Sir Henry Williams Baker
> Hymn [1868]

O beautiful for spacious skies,
For amber waves of grain,
For purple mountain majesties
Above the fruited plain!
America! America!
God shed his grace on thee
And crown thy good with brother-
  hood
From sea to shining sea!

> Katharine Lee Bates
> "America the Beautiful" [1893], st. 1

I have fallen in love with American
  names
The sharp names that never get fat,
The snakeskin titles of mining
  claims,
The plumed war bonnet of Medicine
  Hat,
Tucson and Deadwood and Lost
  Mule Flat.

> Stephen Vincent Benét
> "American Names" [1927], st. 1

God bless America,
Land that I love . . .
From the mountains to the prairies,
To the oceans white with foam,
God bless America,
My home sweet home!

> Irving Berlin
> "God Bless America" [1938]

Make a joyful noise unto the Lord,
  all ye lands.
Serve the Lord with gladness: come
  before his presence with singing.
Know ye that the Lord he is God: it
  is he that hath made us, and not
  we ourselves; we are his people,
  and the sheep of his pasture.
Enter into his gates with thanksgiv-
  ing, and into his courts with
  praise: be thankful unto him, and
  bless his name.
For the Lord is good; his mercy is
  everlasting; and his truth en-
  dureth to all generations.

> Old Testament
> Psalm 100

He only is my rock and my salva-
  tion: he is my defense; I shall not
  be moved.

> The Bible
> Old Testament
> Psalm 62:6

Thou art my hope in the day of evil.

Old Testament
Jeremiah 17:17

Thou shalt love the Lord thy God
with all thine heart, and with all
thy soul, and with all thy might.
And these words, which I command
thee this day, shall be in thine
heart:
And thou shalt teach them dili-
gently unto thy children.

Old Testament
Deuteronomy 6:5–7

They that wait upon the Lord shall
renew their strength; they shall
mount up with wings as eagles;
they shall run, and not be weary,
and they shall walk, and not faint.

Old Testament
Isaiah 40:31

All things work together for good to
them that love God.

> New Testament
> Romans 8:28

For God hath not given us the spirit
of fear; but of power, and of love,
and of a sound mind.

> New Testament
> II Timothy 1:7

Put on the whole armor of God.

> New Testament
> Ephesians 6:11

Set your affection on things above,
not on things on the earth.

> New Testament
> Colossians 3:2

The kingdom of God is within you.

> New Testament
> Luke 17:21

I love all beauteous things,
I seek and adore them;
God hath no better praise,
And man in his hasty days
Is honored for them.

> Robert Bridges
> *Shorter Poems*, bk. IV [1890], no. 1,
> st. 1

Love not Pleasure; love God.

> Thomas Carlyle
> *Sartor Resartus* [1833–1834], bk. II,
> ch. 9

•

We are of course a nation of differences. Those differences don't
make us weak. They're the source
of our strength. . . . The question
is not when we came here . . . but
why our families came here. And
what we did after we arrived.

> Jimmy Carter
> Speech at Al Smith Dinner, New York
> City [October 21, 1976]

He prayeth well who loveth well
Both man and bird and beast.

> Samuel Taylor Coleridge
> *The Rime of the Ancient Mariner*
> [1798], pt. VII, st. 22

He prayeth best who loveth best
All things both great and small;
For the dear God who loveth us,
He made and loveth all.

> Coleridge
> Ibid. st. 23

O happy living things! no tongue
Their beauty might declare:
A spring of love gushed from my
   heart,
And I blessed them unaware.

> Coleridge
> Ibid. pt. IV, st. 14

O the one life within us and abroad,
Which meets all motion and becomes its soul,
A light in sound, a sound-like power in light,
Rhythm in all thought, and joyance everywhere —
Methinks, it should have been impossible
Not to love all things in a world so filled.

Coleridge
"The Eolian Harp" [1795], l. 26

The Infinite Goodness has such wide arms that it takes whatever turns to it.

Dante Alighieri
The Divine Comedy [c. 1310–1321].
Purgatorio, canto III, l. 121

And in His will is our peace.

Dante
Ibid. Paradiso, canto III, l. 85

The Love that moves the sun and
the other stars.

> Dante
> Ibid. Paradiso, canto XXXIII, l. 145

Our country! In her intercourse
with foreign nations may she
always be in the right; but our
country, right or wrong.

> Stephen Decatur
> Toast given at Norfolk [April 1816].
> From A. S. Mackenzie, *Life of
> Stephen Decatur* [1848]

In love of home, the love of country
has its rise.

> Charles Dickens
> *The Old Curiosity Shop* [1841], ch. 38

I never saw a Moor —
I never saw the Sea —
Yet know I how the Heather looks
And what a Billow be.

I never spoke with God
Nor visited in Heaven
Yet chertain am I of the spot
As if the Checks were given —

> Dickinson
> No. 1052 [c. 1865]

I died for Beauty — but was scarce
Adjusted in the Tomb
When One who died for Truth, was
  lain
In an adjoining Room —

> Emily Dickinson
> No. 449 [c. 1862], st. 1

No man is an island, entire of itself;
every man is a piece of the conti-
nent, a part of the main; if a clod
be washed away by the sea, Eu-
rope is the less, as well as if a
promontory were, as well as if a
manor of thy friends or of thine
own were; any man's death diminishes me, because I am in-
volved in mankind; and therefore
never send to know for whom the
bell tolls; it tolls for thee.

> John Donne
> *Devotions upon Emergent Occasions*
> [1624], 17

The Lord God is subtle, but malicious he is not.

> Albert Einstein
> Inscription in Fine Hall, Princeton
> University

I was in love with the whole world
and all that lived in its rainy arms.

> Louise Erdrich
> *Love Medicine* [1984]. The Good Tears

Love is he, radiant with great splendor,
And speaks to us of Thee, O Most
High.

> Saint Francis of Assisi
> "The Song of Brother Sun and of All
> His Creatures" [1225]

Our country is the world — our
countrymen are all mankind.

William Lloyd Garrison
Motto of *The Liberator* [1831]

Lord, make me an instrument of
Your peace. Where there is hatred let me sow love; where there
is injury, pardon; where there is
doubt, faith; where there is despair, hope; where there is darkness, light; and where there is
sadness, joy.
O divine Master, grant that I may
not so much seek to be consoled
as to console; to be understood as
to understand; to be loved as to
love. For it is in giving that we
receive; it is in pardoning that we
are pardoned; and it is in dying
that we are born to eternal life.

Saint Francis of Assisi
Attributed

For he might have been a Roosian,
A French or Turk or Proosian,
Or perhaps Itali-an.
But in spite of all temptations
To belong to other nations,
He remains an Englishman.

> Sir William S. Gilbert
> *H.M.S. Pinafore* [1878], act II

I only regret that I have but one life
   to lose for my country.

> Nathan Hale
> Last words, before being hanged by the
>   British as a spy [September 22, 1776]

To rejoice in life, to find the world
   beautiful and delightful to live in,
   was a mark of the Greek spirit
   which distinguished it from all
   that had gone before. It is a vital
   distinction.

> Edith Hamilton
> *The Greek Way* [1930], ch. 1

All things counter, original, spare,
   strange;
   Whatever is fickle, freckled (who
   knows how?)
   With swift, slow; sweet, sour;
   adazzle, dim;
He fathers-forth whose beauty is past
   change: Praise him.

> Gerard Manley Hopkins
> *Poems* [1918]. No. 37, Pied Beauty,
> l. 7

How to keep — is there any any, is
   there none such, nowhere known
   some, bow or brooch or braid or
   brace, lace, latch or catch or key
   to keep
Back beauty, keep it, beauty,
   beauty, beauty . . . from vanishing
   away?

> Hopkins
> *Poems* [1918], no. 59, The Leaden
> Echo and the Golden Echo

I am willing to love all mankind,
   except an American.

> Samuel Johnson
> From James Boswell, *Life of Johnson*
> [1791], April 15, 1778.

And so, my fellow Americans, ask not what your country can do for you; ask what you can do for your country.

John F. Kennedy
Inaugural address [January 20, 1961]

God sufficeth me: there is no God but He. In Him I put my trust.

The Koran, ch. 9, verse 129

He who loves the world as his body may be entrusted with the empire.

Lao-tzu
The Way of Lao-tzu, 13

To be happy one must be (*a*) well
fed, unhounded by sordid cares,
at ease in Zion, (*b*) full of a com-
fortable feeling of superiority to
the masses of one's fellow men,
and (*c*) delicately and unceas-
ingly amused according to one's
taste. It is my contention that, if
this definition be accepted, there
is no country in the world
wherein a man constituted as I
am — a man of my peculiar
weakness, vanities, appetites, and
aversions — can be so happy as
he can be in the United States.

> H. L. Mencken
> *On Being an American* [1922]

The world stands out on either side
No wider than the heart is wide;
Above the world is stretched the
   sky —
No higher than the soul is high.
The heart can push the sea and land
Farther away on either hand;
The soul can split the sky in two,
And let the face of God shine
   through.

> Edna St. Vincent Millay
> "Renascence" [1912]

O world, I cannot hold thee close
   enough!

> Millay
> "God's World" [1917]

My country is the world and my
   religion is to do good.

> Thomas Paine
> *The Rights of Man*, pt. II [1791], ch. 5

I love the Americans because they
   love liberty, and I love them for
   the noble efforts they made in the
   last war.

> William Pitt, Earl of Chatham
> Speech in the House of Lords [March
>   2, 1770]

This royal throne of kings, this scepter'd isle,
This earth of majesty, this seat of Mars,
This other Eden, demi-paradise,
This fortress built by Nature for herself
Against infection and the hand of war,
This happy breed of men, this little world,
This precious stone set in the silver sea,
Which serves it in the office of a wall,
Or as a moat defensive to a house,
Against the envy of less happier lands,
This blessed plot, this earth, this realm, this England.

> William Shakespeare
> *King Richard the Second*, act II, sc. i, l. 40

Breathes there the man, with soul so dead,
Who never to himself hath said,
This is my own, my native land!
Whose heart hath ne'er within him burn'd
As home his footsteps he hath turn'd
From wandering on a foreign strand!

> Sir Walter Scott
> *The Lay of the Last Minstrel* [1805], canto VI, st. 1

Not that I loved Caesar less, but
that I loved Rome more.

Shakespeare
Julius Caesar, act III, sc. ii, l. 22

I am not an Athenian or a Greek,
but a citizen of the world.

Socrates
From Plutarch, *Of Banishment*

When an American says that he
loves his country, he . . . means
that he loves an inner air, an inner light in which freedom lives
and in which a man can draw the
breath of self-respect.

Adlai E. Stevenson
Speech at New York City [August 27,
1952]

The world is so full of a number of
things,
I'm sure we should all be as happy as
kings.

Robert Louis Stevenson
Ibid. Happy Thought

America is a land of wonders, in which everything is in constant motion and every change seems an improvement. The idea of novelty is there indissolubly connected with the idea of amelioration.

Alexis de Tocqueville
Democracy in America, pt. I [1835], ch. 18

Swiftly arose and spread around me the peace and knowledge
  that pass all the argument of the earth,
And I know that the hand of God is the promise of my own,
And I know that the spirit of God is the brother of my own,
And that all the men ever born are also my brothers, and the
  women my sisters and lovers,
And that a kelson of the creation is love.

Walt Whitman
Leaves of Grass [1891–1892]. Song of Myself, 5